RAISING
PG KIDS
IN AN X-Rated
SOCIETY

EXPLICIT MATERIAL — PARENTAL ADVISORY

TIPPER GORE

RAISING PG KIDS IN AN X-Rated SOCIETY

Abingdon Press • Nashville

RAISING PG KIDS IN AN X-RATED SOCIETY

Copyright © 1987 by Mary Elizabeth Gore

Second Printing 1987

This book is printed on acid-free paper.

Library of Congress Cataloging-in-Publication Data

GORE, TIPPER, 1948-
Raising PG kids in an X-rated society.

Bibliography: p.
Includes index.
1. Mass media and children—United States.
2. Sex in mass media—United States.   3. Violence in mass media—United States.   4. Child rearing—United States.   I. Title.
HQ784.M3G67   1987   302.2'34'088054   87-1813

ISBN 0-687-35283-5 (alk. paper) (cloth)
ISBN 0-687-35282-7 (pbk. : alk. paper)

The quotation from I Corinthians in chapter 3 is from the Revised Standard Version of the Bible, copyrighted 1946, 1952, © 1971, 1973 by the Division of Christian Education of the National Council of the Churches of Christ in the U.S.A., and is used by permission.

Book design by Thelma Whitworth

Manufactured by the Parthenon Press at
Nashville, Tennessee, United States of America

For my husband Al, our parents, and our children.

Contents

Acknowledgments

I would like to express my deep appreciation to my editor, Michael Lawrence. I am also indebted to Lee Ranck for his technical assistance, as well as to Jolie Frantz, Jeff Ling, Jennie Norwood, Carter Eskew, Bob Kanuth, Rebecca Marnhout, and Albert Gore, Sr.

Special thanks to Colette Sweers, Brenda Pearl, and Arnold and Mabel Bollenbacher.

I am especially grateful to Liza McClenaghan for her research and assistance, to Sally Nevius and Pam Howar for their friendship, and to Susan Baker for her loving support and encouragement.

Introduction

Like many parents of my generation, I grew up listening to rock music and loving it, watching television and being entertained by it. I still enjoy both. But something has happened since the days of "Twist and Shout" and "I Love Lucy."

This is a book about the kinds of violent and explicit messages our children are receiving through the media and what we as parents can do about it.

I decided to get involved because I began to see the kinds of record lyrics that my children were being exposed to. It shocked me and made me angry. I started looking deeper into the problem, and became even more concerned.

A small but immensely successful minority of performers have pioneered the "porn rock" phenomenon. A Judas Priest song about oral sex at gunpoint sold two million copies. So did Mötley Crüe's album *Shout at the Devil*, with lyrics like: "Not a woman, but a whore/I can taste the hate/Well, now I'm killing you/Watch your face turning blue."[1] Sheena Easton's "Sugar Walls," about female sexual arousal, was an even bigger hit on Top 40 radio stations. And Prince peddled more than ten million copies of *Purple Rain*, which included a song about a young girl masturbating in a hotel lobby.

This kind of rock music is only part of an escalating trend toward the use of more explicit sex and graphic violence in entertainment industry offerings, from movies and videos to jeans and perfume ads. Music is the most unexpected medium, and rock music has shown perhaps the least willingness to exercise self-restraint.

But in virtually every medium, the communications industry offers increasingly explicit images of sex and violence to younger and younger children. In the course of my work, I've encountered a degree of callousness toward children that I never imagined existed. No one asks what is in the product or its effect on kids, only how well it will sell.

The dilemma for society is how to preserve personal and family values in a nation of diverse tastes. Tensions exist in any free society. But the freedom we enjoy rests on a foundation of individual liberty and shared moral values. Even as the shifting structure of the family and other social changes disrupt old patterns, we must reassert our values through individual and community action. People of all political persuasions—conservatives, moderates, and liberals alike—need to dedicate themselves once again to preserving the moral foundation of our society.

Censorship is not the answer. In the long run, our only hope is for more information and awareness, so that citizens and communities can fight back against market exploitation and find practical means for restoring individual choice and control.

As parents and as consumers, we have the right and the power to pressure the entertainment industry to respond to our needs. Americans, after all, should insist that every corporate giant—whether it produces chemicals or records—accept responsibility for what it produces.

Let me apologize in advance for the profane language and disturbing images that appear throughout this book. These examples are used to expose the material for what it is. I believe that the current excesses could not and would not have developed if more people had been aware of them. Unfortunately, many parents remain unaware of the indecent liberties some entertainers take with their children. Perhaps full disclosure will stir parents to try to stop the wholesale exploitation of American youth.

More than anything else, I want this book to be a call to arms for American parents. I want to offer them the very real hope that we can reassert some control over the cultural environment in which our children are raised.

Tipper Gore
Carthage, Tennessee

1

A Mother Takes a Stand

You say that things are getting out of hand. This is an inflammatory statement. . . . Rock and roll has always meant sex. . . . But maybe it's not fucking that you're against; maybe it's just masturbation that you find offensive.

—rock singer Wendy O. Williams[1]

As the fatigue from the day's events settled in, while I waited at LaGuardia Airport, I couldn't stop my mind from replaying the hostile confrontation I had just experienced. Now I was alone in New York City, stranded by stormy weather. This was one of the worst nights of my life.

I had just endured three hours of verbal attacks from angry rock stars and other recording artists. The New York Chapter of the National Association of Recording Arts & Sciences (NARAS), which presents the coveted Grammy Awards, had invited me to represent the Parents' Music Resource Center in a panel on explicit lyrics. I knew that some songwriters and performers in NARAS did not especially appreciate our views, but they needed to hear how a number of consumers feel about certain musicians' products. I thought I could help them understand our concerns.

I never had a chance. The panel included record producer Bob Porter, jazz artist Mtume, and punk rock singer Wendy O. Williams, in a T-shirt emblazoned with the words "Eat Your Honey." The

15

audience consisted of a business associate of the rock group Twisted Sister, punk rockers sporting purple mohawk haircuts and T-shirts bearing the logo for the heavy metal band Venom, and a few quiet NARAS officials. Every question, for almost three hours, was aimed at me. Many were highly personal and insulting. No doubt about it—I had been set up.

I suggested to the panel that parents have a right to know what their children are buying and hearing. Wendy O. Williams, a Grammy nominee, replied that I was upset about these songs simply because I can't handle the possibility that my own child might masturbate. "When is it all right for a child to masturbate . . . Mrs. Gore?" she asked.

Ms. Williams obviously considered me a neurotic Washington housewife who dislikes sex. She proceeded to read from the Song of Solomon and *Twelfth Night*. It almost seemed worth the pain to hear a woman who sings songs like "(Work That Muscle) F**K That Booty" recite the Bible and Shakespeare.

How could these people, prominent in their fields, be so insensitive? Perhaps naïvely, I had expected reasonable people to spiritedly disagree. But it never occurred to me that record industry officials would be a party to such tasteless personal attacks. Nor did I imagine that the people who play a role in awarding Grammys would refuse to take explicit lyrics seriously. If these are the folks who hand out the music awards, no wonder we're having problems.

As the panel concluded, a woman asked if I would have accepted the invitation had I known that everyone was going to be against me. "Yes," I answered as calmly as I could, "I am pleased to discuss the issue—and to exercise my First Amendment rights."

I rushed to the airport, only to learn that all flights to Washington had been canceled. I had never felt so alone. It had been a long and hard day, and I was angry and perplexed. I longed for the familiarity, love, and comfort of home! How had I gotten myself into this situation?

FORMATION OF THE PMRC

I had become aware of the emergence of explicit and violent images in the world of music several months earlier, through my children. In December 1984, I purchased Prince's best-selling album *Purple Rain* for my eleven-year-old daughter. I had seen Prince on the cover of magazines, and I knew that he was the biggest pop idol in years. My daughter wanted his album because she had heard the single "Let's Go Crazy" on the radio. But when we brought the album home, put it on our stereo, and listened to it together, we heard the words to another song, "Darling Nikki": "I knew a girl named Nikki/Guess [you] could say she was a sex fiend/I met her in a hotel lobby/Masturbating with a magazine."[2] The song went on and on, in a similar manner. I couldn't believe my ears! The vulgar lyrics embarrassed both of us. At first, I was stunned—then I got mad! Millions of Americans were buying *Purple Rain* with no idea what to expect. Thousands of parents were giving the album to their children—many even younger than my daughter.

Around that time, my two younger daughters, ages six and eight, began asking me about things they had seen on MTV, the music video channel on cable television. I had always thought that videos had great potential as a dramatic new art form, but I had not watched many. I began watching more often, and I observed that several included adult (or at least "mature") themes and images. "Mom, why is the teacher taking off her clothes?" my six-year-old asked, after watching Van Halen's *Hot for Teacher,* in which a "teacher" does a striptease act for the boys in her class.

I sat down with my kids and watched videos like Mötley Crüe's *Looks That Kill,* with scantily clad women being captured and imprisoned in cages by a studded-leather–clad male band. In *Photograph,* by Def Leppard, we saw a dead woman tied up with barbed wire. The Scorpions' *Rock You Like a Hurricane* showed a man tied to the walls of a torture chamber and a singer being choked by a woman.[3] These images frightened my children; they frightened *me!* The graphic sex and the violence were too much for us to handle.

Other parents were experiencing the same rude awakening. One day in early 1985, my friend Susan Baker came by to talk about her concerns. Susan and her husband, U.S. Treasury Secretary James Baker, have eight children. She told me that two of her friends were getting ready to take action on the issue of pornographic and violent images in music, and asked if I would be interested in signing a letter inviting others to a meeting to hear more about the excesses in some rock music.

18

I was so angry about the songs my children and I had heard that I quickly agreed to join Susan Baker in doing something about it. Susan was working with Sally Nevius, a former dean of admissions at Mount Vernon College in Washington. Sally and her husband, the former chairman of the District of Columbia City Council, had an eleven-year-old daughter. Also assisting Susan Baker was Pam Howar, a businesswoman with a seven-year-old daughter.

We decided to establish the nonprofit Parents' Music Resource Center, to be known as the PMRC. In May of 1985, we set out to alert other parents in our community. Sally arranged for Jeff Ling, a former rock musician who is now a youth minister at a suburban Virginia church, to give a slide presentation graphically illustrating the worst excesses in rock music, from lyrics to concert performances to rock magazines aimed at the teenage market. We invited the public, community leaders, our friends (some of whom hold public office), and representatives of the music industry. Our hope was to generate a discussion of the issue, raise public awareness, and begin a dialogue with people in the industry. To our surprise, more than 350 people showed up at our first meeting on May 15, 1985, at St. Columba's Church in Washington, D.C.

To my knowledge, no music industry representatives attended this meeting, with one very important exception: Eddie Fritts, president of the National Association of Broadcasters (NAB), unable to attend himself, had sent his wife, Martha Dale Fritts, and two NAB staff members. They brought with them a letter that Mr. Fritts had just written and sent to eight hundred group station owners, which alerted them to growing concern among the public over "porn rock":

> The lyrics of some recent rock records and the tone of their related music videos are fast becoming a matter of public debate. The subject has drawn national attention through articles in publications like *Newsweek* and *USA Today* and feature reports on TV programs like "Good Morning, America."
>
> Many state that they are extremely troubled by the sexually explicit and violent language of some of today's songs. . . .
>
> The pre-teen and teen audiences are heavy listeners, viewers and buyers of rock music. In some communities, like Washington, D.C., parents and other interested citizens are organizing to see what they can do about the music in question, which at least one writer has dubbed "porn rock."
>
> I wanted you, as one of the leaders in the broadcasting industry, to be aware of this situation. . . .
>
> It is, of course, up to each broadcast licensee to make its own decisions as to the manner in which it carries out its programming responsibilities under the Communications Act.

Two weeks later, Mr. Fritts wrote to the heads of forty-five major record companies:

> At its May meeting, NAB's Executive Committee asked that I write you to request that all recordings made available to broadcasters in the future be accompanied by copies of the songs' lyrics. It appears that providing this material to broadcasters would place very little burden on the recording industry,

while greatly assisting the decision making of broadcast management and programming staffs.

Eddie Fritts has a keen sense of corporate responsibility. He and his wife also have teenagers at home. Many station owners and programmers share his concerns. In June 1985, the industry newspaper *Radio and Records* reported: "Record industry officials declined comment, but radio programmers spotchecked by *R&R* this week generally welcomed the NAB's suggestion that record companies enclose written lyrics with records to help stations detect sexually explicit or violent wordings that may be inappropriate for their audiences." The story quoted Guy Zapoleon of Phoenix, who said: "I think it's an excellent idea. We have a responsibility to our audience to watch the wordings on songs. Without wanting to sound prudish, I think we owe it to the public to be careful."[4]

Record companies were not so excited. Lenny Waronker, president of Warner Brothers Records (Prince's label), rejected the NAB request to include lyrics. "It smells of censorship," he told the *Los Angeles Times*. "Rock and roll over the years has always had these little . . . furors. Radio stations can make their own decisions about what they want to play." A representative of one local station, the sometimes controversial KROQ-FM in Pasadena, California, agreed: "It's freedom of choice. The music is the beat; the lyrics come secondary. . . . We make our money on sex, from A to Z. It's what sells."[5]

Considering the initial NAB response, we were off to a good start, but what should we do next? How could we make ourselves heard by the giants of the record industry, like Warner Brothers, Capitol, and RCA?

A SECRET ALLY

By happy chance, we gained an ally in the recording industry who could help us find our way through the music business. Throughout the ensuing campaign, he gave us invaluable advice—on the condition that he never be identified.

Our secret ally held an important position in the record industry. Like us, he was sickened and disgusted by the trend toward pornography and violence in some rock music. He advised us to set up a meeting with Stan Gortikov at the Recording Industry Association of America (RIAA), the trade group that represents all major record companies. Gortikov had been president of the RIAA since 1972, and before that he had headed Capitol Records. He agreed to meet with us in early June.

Our strategy was simple. We felt it was crucial to publicize the excesses in song lyrics and videos, the source of our concern. We were convinced that most parents are either unaware of the trends in rock music, or uncertain what to do about them. We decided to get the word out and build a consumer movement to put pressure on the industry. From the start, we recognized that the only solution would involve some voluntary action on the part of the industry. We wanted industry leaders to assume direct corporate responsibility for their products. The problem was to persuade an industry profiting from excesses to exercise some self-restraint.

22

In 1984, the National Congress of Parents and Teachers (the National PTA) had called on record companies to label their products for sexual content, violence, and profanity, in order to inform parents about inappropriate materials. The PTA had written to thirty-two record companies but had only received three responses. And those refused to discuss the issue further. Our ally advised us not to deal with the companies on an individual basis.

He suggested that we present our plans to the RIAA's Gortikov and not leave him any choice. Our source said the best way to catch the industry's attention was on the airwaves. So the PRMC launched a grass-roots media campaign that soon took on a life of its own.

FROM NEWS STORY TO NATIONAL ISSUE

From June to November 1985, we held dozens of meetings, participated in frequent conference calls, and exchanged numerous letters, as we sought solutions palatable to the industry and to the National PTA and the PMRC. As our negotiations intensified, the issue quickly became a national one.

Media coverage of the campaign included well over 150 newspaper columns, editorials, and radio stories about the porn rock issue. Ellen Goodman, William Raspberry, George Will, Charles Krauthammer, William Shannon, Judy Mann, Mike Royko, David Gergen, and many other syndicated columnists wrote favorable reviews. Reuter's North European Service carried stories, while the BBC did separate radio and TV interviews with Susan Baker and me. *The Economist* of London, the *Wall Street Journal,*

U.S. News & World Report, Esquire, Newsweek, Newsday, The New Republic, the *New York Times,* the *Los Angeles Times,* and *USA Today* all ran stories. Most were supportive. "The difference between the music of yesteryear and that of today is the leap one makes from swimsuits in *Sports Illustrated* to the centerfolds of *Hustler,*" David Gergen wrote in *U.S. News & World Report.* "If an album were X-rated, most radio stations and video programs would drop the worst offenders."[6]

The media campaign took care of itself. A small story about our first public meeting appeared in the "Style" section of the *Washington Post.* Before we knew it, we were besieged with requests for interviews. Kandy Stroud, a journalist, musician, and mother of three, had earlier written a "My Turn" column entitled "Stop Pornographic Rock" for the May 6, 1985, edition of *Newsweek.* She immediately received an invitation to appear on "Good Morning, America." Kandy and Pam Howar appeared on "Panorama," a Washington television show. Soon after that, I did an hour-long radio talk show in Oklahoma City, and Susan Baker and Sally Nevius participated in a similar show in another state.

News of the PMRC's fight to alert the public to porn rock spread quickly. The women of the PMRC collectively did hundreds of interviews on radio and television and for magazines and newspapers across the country and around the world. The "Donahue Show," "Today," "CBS Morning News," PBS's "Late Night America," all three networks' evening news shows, "Entertainment Tonight," "Hour Magazine," and many others picked up the story.

Meanwhile, Mr. Gortikov of the RIAA gave us a crash course on the recording industry. In a meeting with the PRMC in June 1985, he explained that the companies in the RIAA sell 85 percent of the recorded music in America. While the industry had considered a rating system, he said it would be too difficult to administer. The movie industry rates about 350 new films a year; the recording industry produces some 25,000 songs and 2,500 albums annually. Gortikov insisted that most recorded music was positive, despite the many "indefensible" examples of "plain bad taste." We assured him that we had no complaint about most rock and roll music, but that something had to be done about the vast commercial excesses.

Gortikov said his hands were tied, but offered to "do my best to exercise persuasion with the record companies; in my correspondence I will start to heighten awareness."

BATTLING "THE WASHINGTON WIVES"

In August, a middle-aged rocker named Frank Zappa, who enjoys a dedicated following, emerged as the record industry spokesperson chosen to confront the PMRC. Zappa labeled us "the Washington wives," and (my personal favorite) "cultural terrorists." He summarized his arguments in *Cash Box* magazine:

> No person married to or related to a government official should be permitted to waste the nation's time on ill-conceived housewife hobby projects such as this.

The PMRC's case is totally without merit, based on a hodge-podge of fundamentalist frogwash and illogical conclusions.[7]

He was not the only one to surface in opposition to the PMRC. With a cry of "Censorship!" Danny Goldberg, president of Gold Mountain Records, formed Musical Majority, which enlisted the help of artists like Daryl Hall and John Cougar Mellencamp. While the Musical Majority defended artists' rights, the PMRC raised questions about the rights of others. What about the right of parents to protect their children? What about the right of citizens not to be bombarded with explicit material in the public domain?

Our opponents tried to dismiss us with sexist comments about housewives trading on their husbands' influence. But they failed to realize that we spoke for millions of other parents who shared these same concerns and who would not be dismissed out of hand.

THE CENSORSHIP SMOKESCREEN

The PMRC proposed a unique mechanism to increase consumer choice in the marketplace instead of limiting it. Our approach was the direct opposite of censorship. We called for more information, not less. We did not advocate a ban of even the most offensive albums or tapes. We simply urged that the consumer be forewarned through the use of warning labels and/or printed lyrics visible on the outside packaging of music products. Critics used the smokescreen of censorship to dodge the real issue, which was lack of any corporate responsibility for the impact their products may have on young people.

The PMRC sought to balance the precious right of artistic free speech with the right of parents to protect their children from explicit messages that they are not mature enough to understand or deal with. These two rights are not mutually exclusive and one should not be sacrificed for the other. Records, tapes, and videos are consumer products, mass-produced, distributed, and marketed to the public. Children and parents of children constitute the bulk of that consuming public.

The PMRC and the National PTA have agreed that these musical products should enjoy all the rights and privileges guaranteed by the First Amendment. But as Thomas Jefferson once said, when excesses occur, the best guarantee of free speech is *more* speech, not less. That's all we asked for—awareness and disclosure. Our proposal amounted to nothing more than truth-in-packaging, a time-honored principle in our free-enterprise system.

In this information age, such consumer information gives parents an important tool for making choices for their children. Without it, parental guidance in the matter of available entertainment is virtually impossible. The PMRC proposal does *not* infringe on the First Amendment. It does *not* raise a constitutional issue. But it *does* seek to reform marketing practices by asking for better and more informative packaging. And it *does* seek to inform consumers when artistic expression borders on what legendary singer Smokey Robinson has called "musical pornography."[8]

Who decides which songs are musical pornography? Only the record company can make that decision—not the government, as some would have us believe, and not an outside censorship board, as others have charged. The music industry, which allowed these excesses to develop, would be asked to take responsibility for the product it markets to the public.

In fact, we are talking about products primarily written for children, marketed to children, and sold to children. In this country we rightly treat children differently from adults; most people feel that children should not enjoy the same access to adult material as adults. Children are not allowed into R-rated movies if they are under seventeen. In most places, minors are not allowed to buy *Playboy* and *Penthouse* or go into adult bookstores.

If no one under eighteen can buy *Penthouse* magazine, why should children be subjected to explicit album covers and lyrics that are even worse? If we have decided it is not in the best interest of society to allow children into X-rated bookstores, why should they be subjected to hard-core porn in the local record shop? A recent album from the Dead Kennedys band contained a graphic poster of multiple erect penises penetrating vaginas. Where's the difference?

In the hands of a few warped artists, their brand of rock music has become a Trojan Horse, rolling explicit sex and violence into our homes. This ruse made us gasp at the cynicism of the recording company executives who control the music business. They found it easy to confuse the issue by throwing out cries of censorship while refusing to address the real problem. They dodged the real point—that in a free society we can affirm the First Amendment and also protect the rights of children and adults who seek to avoid the twisted tyranny of explicitness in the public domain.

PROPOSING ALTERNATIVES TO THE MUSIC INDUSTRY

At a second meeting with the RIAA's Stan Gortikov, on May 31, 1985, we presented a letter to him signed by sixteen wives of United States representatives and senators:

It is our concern that some of the music which the recording industry sells today increasingly portrays explicit sex and violence, and glorifies the use of drugs and alcohol. It is indiscriminately available to persons of any age through record stores and the media.

These messages reach young children and early teenagers at a crucial age when they are developing lifelong value systems. Their minds are often not yet discerning enough to reject the destructive influences and anti-social behaviour engendered by what they hear and see in these products.

Because of the excesses that exist in the music industry today, we petition the industry to exercise voluntary self-restraint perhaps by developing guidelines and/or a rating system, such as that of the movie industry, for use by parents in order to protect our younger children from such mature themes.

Braced with this letter, Mr. Gortikov pledged to work swiftly within the music industry.

Over the next few months, we negotiated several alternatives with the RIAA. We began by asking for a categorical rating system based on content, then suggested using the symbol "R" to designate explicit albums. Finally, we joined forces with the National PTA and its 5.8 million members. Together with the RIAA we called for a consumer warning label on explicit or violent albums or for full disclosure of lyrics. "We recommend this course of action because we believe it protects consumers by providing them with valuable information while respecting recording artists' First Amendment rights," said National PTA president Ann Kahn.[9]

Pam Howar of the PMRC urged the industry to "create a uniform standard to be used to define what constitutes blatant, explicit lyric content."[10] We thought the ideal solution would be a label (or some symbol) to advise the consumer about explicit lyrics in a particular album. Printed lyrics would also enable the consumer to make an informed decision appropriate for their child's age. Since most albums would not concern parents, there had to be some way to flag those that might.

As our critics were quick to note, some album covers are explicit enough in themselves to show they are unsuitable for children. But many albums with inoffensive covers include explicit lyrics. We suggested distributing a master lyric sheet to all retail stores, but Gortikov said there would be too many outlets to cover and keep up to date. It seemed that the only solution was to attach the lyric sheet directly to the product. We wondered if sheets of explicit and violent lyrics might actually attract children. But the National PTA's Ann Kahn insisted that it would be best to address explicit lyrics with more openness, not less. That approach seems to best balance artists' right of free expression with consumers' right to know what they are buying.

While we were calling publicly for consumer warning labels on albums containing explicit lyrics, and for an industry panel to set guidelines defining explicit material, we worked feverishly behind the scenes to obtain industry endorsement of a uniform standard—one written by the industry itself, not by us. The standard would loosely define what constituted blatantly explicit lyric content. Meanwhile, the Musical Majority and others lined up pop stars to blast "music censorship" and the women who would "ban rock and roll." Our ally in the industry had warned us that we would be no match for prominent artists calling us "censoring prudes" or worse, as industry leaders fought to protect the status quo and their economic interests.

Reprinted by permission: Tribune Media Services

THE SENATE HEARING

By this time, the United States Congress had begun to take an interest in the issue, and many members considered holding hearings. In September 1985, Senator John Danforth of Missouri scheduled a hearing before the Senate's commerce committee, which he chaired. The commerce committee has jurisdiction over communications issues, and wanted to investigate the prevalence of pornographic, violent rock lyrics for its own information—not to consider any legislation.

The hearing put me in an awkward position because my husband, Albert Gore, Jr., was a freshman member of the commerce committee. Some critics mistakenly assumed that he had asked for the hearing, when in fact, both he and I had had reservations about it. I thought the PMRC would be better off working with artists and the industry on their own terms, instead of dragging everybody before the TV cameras on Capitol Hill. Artists were already screaming about censorship, and this would only give them an excuse to raise the specter of government intervention.

However, our industry source welcomed the idea. In his view, it would take congressional attention to make the record industry budge. His only regret was that Senator Danforth let the executives know in advance that no legislation would come out of it.

In any event, the September 19 hearing certainly brought the issue out for public debate. It turned out to be the most widely publicized media event in congressional history. A seat in the hearing room was the hottest ticket in town all year.

Both sides turned out in force. Susan Baker and I testified for the PMRC, and Jeff Ling gave his slide show. The National PTA also sent representatives who testified. Frank Zappa, John Denver, and Dee Snider of Twisted Sister also appeared.

The hearing did not seek to reach any consensus, but on the whole we were pleased to see the facts come out. Twisted Sister's Dee Snider told the committee that he was a Christian who did not smoke, drink, or do drugs, and insisted that he had been unfairly accused. A member of the committee—my husband—asked him the full name of his fan club, SMF Fans of Twisted Sister. Replied Snider, "It stands for Sick Mother Fucking Fans of Twisted Sister."[11]

AGREEMENT WITH THE RIAA

After the Senate hearing, the negotiations produced results that all parties felt represented a workable and fair arrangement. We decided to make a major compromise—to accept the formation of an RIAA policy statement on explicit lyrics, and drop our request for a uniform standard of what is or is not explicit. We would also drop our request for an R rating on albums or tapes to designate explicit products, in exchange for the warning "Explicit Lyrics—Parental Advisory." We agreed to give the compromise a chance to work in the marketplace, and to monitor it jointly and assess its effectiveness a year later. We also agreed to cease the media campaign for one year. On November 1, 1985, the RIAA, the National PTA, and the PMRC jointly announced the agreement at the National Press Club in Washington.

The critics, of course, weren't finished. I became the victim of harsh and often tasteless attacks. Someone sent me a copy of *SPIN*, a music magazine published by Bob Guccione, Jr., and financed by his father, the publisher of *Penthouse*.[12] It contained a satirical article entitled "Tipper Gore's Diary," which detailed all the songs I would ban before or after lunch. The article eventually raised itself to the level of a personal pornographic attack, by alluding in rather uncivilized terms to my sexual relations with my husband.[13] *Hustler*, a pornographic magazine, also crowned me "Asshole of the Month."

"KIDS CAN'T WRITE LETTERS LIKE THESE"

In the midst of this rather frenzied activity my third-grade daughter, Kristin, came into my room one evening and said, "Oh, Mom, we made some man really mad that we wrote him letters."

"Oh," I said, at this point thoroughly prepared for almost anything (or so I thought).

"Yeah, really mad, he called up the school and everything."

I said, "Kristin, will you ask your teacher to call me when it's convenient?"

The next day the school principal told me what had happened. The phone had rung and an angry voice had demanded to speak to the principal. "I'm from the National Association of Broadcasters and I want to know the meaning of these letters! (This was not NAB president Eddie Fritts; it was a staff member. In fact, Mr. Fritts later wrote a lovely letter to the children.) The caller had continued: "I don't believe that kids could write letters like these! Some teacher must have put 'em up to it. Kid's couldn't know about these things!" The principal described him as ranting and raving.

Actually the children of this third-grade class had read a lead story in their newspaper, the *Scholastic News*, about the record rating issue. The author invited them to write down their feelings and thoughts about the issue and send them to officials.[14] The teacher had asked Kristin to see if I would come in one morning and answer their questions. I did. Their questions were very good, covering the whole range of concerns, from the artists' rights to the raunch and violence in some songs and videos to what their parents and siblings thought and did about such media exposure. These tuned-in kids then wrote very sensible letters.

The man from the NAB apparently didn't know that eight-year-olds listen to the radio, watch rock videos, and can think and express themselves remarkably well. In fact, they often make more sense on this issue than many adults—and they are polite. It is fascinating to hear them discuss in their own words what they hear and see, because they clearly perceive the sex, the explicitness of some of the images and words, and they are very aware of the extreme violence of some of the videos. They call the merger of violence and sex "yucky" and "gross."

Ironically, the NAB man was unaware that a New

York disc jockey has called MTV a seductive "Sesame Street" teaching all the wrong values.[15] He must have also missed Ellen Goodman's column on the little "Wanna Be's,"—eight-, nine-, and ten-year-olds who copy Madonna right down to the lace bra.[16] He also missed Dee Snider's statement in a teen fan magazine about greeting the increasingly younger fans of his band, Twisted Sister, with "Alright you sick motherfuckers, if you're ready to kick some ass, we're Twisted-fuckin'-Sister!"[17]

Apparently the man from the NAB missed the fact that Twisted Sister is so popular with youngsters tuned into MTV that MTV had offered a day with Dee Snider as a prize in a "Back to School" contest they sponsored. I didn't discuss such things with the third graders. I didn't have to introduce them to Twisted Sister. They already knew about that group, and Mötley Crüe, and Judas Priest.

"Someone must have talked to them," the NAB man said, "someone must have put them up to this."

"Well, Mrs. Gore's daughter is in the class and Mrs. Gore did speak to them," the principal explained; "we encourage our children to get involved and to learn how to be good citizens."

That really set him off. "He is really angry at you," the principal told me. "He said something about an agreement on November 1 and these letters were dated November 15 and you weren't supposed to discuss this anymore." She paused. "He said the issue has been settled."

Talk about reverence for the First Amendment! Talk about censorship! This man from the National Association of Broadcasters raved at my daughter's

school principal because I had violated some imagined gag order in answering the questions of third
graders who were in the pursuit of knowledge. What a
turn of events. But he didn't stop there. He asked the
principal if the parents knew that their children were
writing such letters. They had used words like "sex"
and "no clothes" and "violence." "I'm sure their
parents wouldn't want them to write these letters,"
he had said.

MAKING COMMUNITY FEELINGS RESPECTED

During October and November of 1985, the New
York-based Simmons Market Research Bureau surveyed the nation on the issue of rating records.
Seventy-five percent of those surveyed agreed there
should be a rating system. Additionally, 80 percent
wanted the lyrics visible on the outside of the albums
or tapes, where they can be read.[18] And the censorship
charge didn't stand up to scrutiny.

I felt particularly gratified when the president of
the American Civil Liberties Union, Norman Dor-
sen, and Harriet Pilpel, co-chair of the National
Coalition Against Censorship, praised the Parents'
Music Resource Center on July 4, 1986, at the Liberty
Conference in New York City. The *New York Times*
said of my presentation:

> The cofounder of the Parent's Music Resource
> Center, Tipper Gore, got a warm response for her
> group's effort to get record companies to identify on
> record jackets the sexually explicit lyrics inside.
> The civil libertarians present liked her approach of
> relying on community pressures rather than legal

37

constraints; of asking not that any record be banned but only that parents be given an opportunity to discover before a purchase was made what their children were buying. [Mrs.] Gore seemed to have found a means of making community feelings respected in a way that also respected the First Amendment.[19]

2

Where Have All the Children Gone?

When I was a child, I spoke like a child, I thought like a child, I reasoned like a child.
—St. Paul, I Corinthians 13:11

Kids are really sophisticated now. They don't need to be sheltered. Little girls wanna be fucked, teenagers, little boys, they wanna fuck. They do!
—Paul Rutherford of the band Frankie Goes to Hollywood[1]

In the debate over explicit materials, some people tend to treat children simply as miniature adults, with mature reasoning powers and critical thinking skills. Adults sometimes forget that children are psychologically unique and have special vulnerabilities and evolving capabilities that change dramatically during successive stages of development and maturation.

Only a few years ago, it was thought that newborns couldn't see or focus their eyes. Now we know that not only can they see, they express a clear preference for certain colors and patterns. Parenting books such as those developed by the Gesell Institute talk about the fears that are prevalent among two-year-olds. These fears change at four, at six, at eight, and at twelve. We should keep that in mind as we examine media presentations for children.

One set of parents told me that their four-year-old had nightmares for a week after watching the music video *Thriller* (which shows Michael Jackson turning into a monster, frightening his girl friend, and joining graveyard ghouls in a great dance routine that older teens love). They didn't know what was the matter, because their child couldn't explain what she saw. Teenagers in the family had watched the video with her. They thought it was funny, but she was terrified and the frightening images lodged in her mind.

Researchers have confirmed what attentive observers of child behavior have known all along: Most children develop emotionally, intellectually, physically, and cognitively according to a certain timetable and along a clearly recognizable path. There is, for example, a specific age in middle childhood when children develop the skills of moral reasoning. Young children don't recognize the conceptual difference between truth and lies until around five years of age. The conscience isn't fully developed and operational until age eight. During these early years of rapid growth and development, children are intimately dependent upon the parents who will be their primary influences until they reach legal adulthood, which our society confers at eighteen. Unfortunately, in our society parents all too often receive very little education about this most important responsibility.

Parents are children's primary advocates and defenders. It is important to convey to the child that support will always be there and that love will not be conditional. At the same time, parents must enforce limits and provide discipline. A structure of loving discipline, limits, and standards of behavior are essential to the child's well-being. We all need to understand more about the mental growth and development of our children. They deserve better than to be treated like miniature adults.

Every child needs the security of knowing where the boundary lines are. He or she will test them at two, again at four, and again at fourteen and sixteen, all in different ways. At each age the loving parent must make adjustments, but continue to provide the security of definable boundaries.

The more parents know about the mind of the child, the better they can protect and nurture the child. Children five and under generally cannot distinguish fantasy from reality on television or in stories. They will be able to tell the difference only when their brains are ready. Teenagers are more complex. They begin to look and talk like adults as early as thirteen, but they are still *children in transition* who need as much time as younger kids.

The teen years are turning points in young lives. Teenagers are endowed with the emotions, passions, and physical capabilities of adults, without the adult judgment to harness them. Because of the pressures they face, they may need even more "quality time" from parents. Teens look to their parents for a moral compass—values and ethical advice they can apply to romances and friendships.

When the teen quest for independence begins, conscientious parents will know their children well enough to give them only as much freedom as they can handle.

The two main stages in adolescence are the struggle for identity, which goes through many cycles and ideally is resolved in the early twenties, and the development of sexual relationships. The developing teen experiences complex physical longings and extremely strong emotions of all kinds.

Teenagers are learning about their bodies, which are undergoing tremendous transformations, their sexuality, and their personalities and how they affect others. They are impressionable, and are especially subject to pressures and temptations from their friends.

Adults should strive to alleviate some of the intense pressures teenagers must face. At a time when they are emotionally unsettled, teens are struggling to cope with a legion of problems: relationships with parents, siblings, and peers; the use of alcohol, tobacco, and drugs; sex, sexually transmitted diseases, and pregnancy; respect for and rebellion against authority; a continuing search for self-identity; questions of faith and personal religious commitment; schoolwork, part-time jobs, and the future. Those are more choices than most adults would care to make.

So anyone who attempts to debate the porn rock issue as if young people are in the same intellectual and emotional category as adults does them a terrible injustice. We need to let children be children. Children think differently from adults, and process information according to their own stages of development. Consequently, adults must not overlook the exaggerated impact that violent and explicit images can have on children, or forget that children are different.

THE CHANGING FAMILY STRUCTURE

Children have always been uniquely vulnerable. But they are even more vulnerable in today's society, for two reasons. Children are now bombarded with explicit messages on a scale unlike anything our culture has ever seen. And American families are undergoing profound changes that are depriving millions of children of the support structure they once enjoyed. As Robert Coles, an author and child psychiatrist at Harvard University, has observed: "If strong family or church life is absent, what other moral influences are there? Children take what they see in movies to be the adult world in operation—they tell you that."[2]

The traditional image of the smiling nuclear family with both parents at home and close relatives nearby now represents less than 7 percent of American families.

A decade from now, the majority of seventeen-year-olds will come from broken homes. The number of families maintained by women alone grew almost

Steve Kelley, The San Diego Union

43

90 percent between 1970 and 1985.[3] The growth is attributed to more divorces and more unwed mothers. By 1980, women headed 56 percent of poor families with children.[4]

Thirteen million children live in single-parent homes,[5] and 59 percent of all children live in a home where both parents or the sole parent is working. Two-thirds of all mothers now work.[6] Congresswoman Sala Burton of San Francisco held hearings on the subject of "latchkey kids": children who come home to empty houses after school. Their numbers are estimated at seven million. At the hearing, one expert on the subject testified that he has found children as young as eighteen months left to care for themselves.[7] Surely these children's parents are in dire straits themselves. But whatever the reason, such children should not be forgotten.

These social changes place a heavy burden on children. They are often thrown into the world of adult problems, with devastating results.

Something is terribly wrong in their lives. They are attempting to replace what is missing, to deal with the inordinate amount of stress that a broken family produces, all at a time when they need as much love and support as they can get. Instead, the reality they must cope with is far different from what their emotional needs would dictate. Many of them are ill equipped to cope. Parents do not do this with malice in their hearts; they are struggling themselves. Yet one can't help feeling most of all for the children. They are the most vulnerable; they are the innocents.

The Education Commission of the States found that almost 2.5 million teens between the ages of sixteen and nineteen were "disconnected from society" and alienated. The business advisory panel of the commission, headed by former Governor Charles Robb of Virginia, reported that this disconnection and alienation was attributable to several factors, the overriding one being the breakdown of the family. The major problem areas for teenagers were identified as the epidemics of pregnancy, suicide, and drug and alcohol abuse. The commission also reported that the teen homicide rate had increased a stunning 232 percent from 1950.[8]

In California, the Governor's Task Force on Youth Gang Violence reported that an estimated fifty thousand teens belong to gangs in the Los Angeles area alone, many of them organized around heavy metal and punk rock music.[9]

Not all the violence our children witness is simulated in the media. Family violence, including spouse abuse and child abuse, is increasing. We are our children's most important influence. We teach them—but what are we teaching?

All these teen troubles suggest that the breakdown of the family and disenchantment with the educational system contribute to the growing alienation of some youth, while traditional support groups are failing to do their jobs. With parental involvement and supervision at an all-time low, many children and teenagers feel they've been set adrift.

The symptoms are frightening: Over five thousand children are killed by their caretakers each year.[10] Each year one million teens run away from home;[11] another million get pregnant;[12] some five thousand commit suicide, while four hundred thousand attempt it;[13] thousands of children are verbally, emotionally, and physically abused in their homes every day. Others are victims of sexual abuse. Nearly two million cases of abuse and neglect were reported in 1985. Some children are lured into cults. Others just go missing, or end up in a simple pauper's grave, never to be identified.

Why does this tear one's heart out so? Why do we feel so much more than simple concern? These emotions are a reaction to the fragility and innocence of children. We feel as we do because we know that children are special gifts and deserve to be treated with love and respect, gentleness and honesty. They deserve security and guidance about living, loving, and relating to other people. And they deserve vigilant protection from the excesses of adult society.

It is about time that we understood these truths—not only as parents but as members of a society and a culture that should show more respect for every child's special vulnerabilities and needs.

3

The Cult of Violence

A conscientious man would be cautious how he dealt in blood.
                                        —Edmund Burke

I like to drink blood out of a skull and torture females on stage.
                        —Blackie Lawless of the band W.A.S.P.[1]

Blackie Lawless is anything but typical of rock musicians. Yet his disturbing message is a sign of the times. While Lawless and others like him may think they are merely entertaining impressionable youth with their shocking rituals, the country is witnessing more and more reports of youth violence and sexual assaults. As a nation, we remain somewhat isolated in our homes and places of work, and many of us are still unaware of the increasing number of violent acts, from murder to deadly assaults, being perpetrated *by young people* in every state. We simply cannot afford to ignore these mounting statistics any longer.

We live in a violent world, and America itself has a history of wars, civil strife, and crime. Humankind is a violent race and is host to aggressive impulses. But the real violence that we do to one another and must learn to control is of our own making, and as such is largely preventable. Its source lies in our families, neighborhoods, and communities, and we must

47

effectively deal with all its causes and focus on its prevention, if we are to survive.

The violence that haunts our society has reached its extreme in the nuclear arms race. Our children grow up beneath a frightening nuclear shadow, the threat of annihilation hanging over them like the sword of Damocles. And all now live with the reality of international terrorism spilling the blood of the innocent. The violence in our lives is also often glorified and commercially exploited in the mass media, and unless we want to continue robbing, beating, maiming, and killing each other, that too presents all of us with a great and important challenge.

Just as it is imperative that we work intelligently to defuse the nuclear threat, so must we come to terms with the unfettered commercial exploitation of violence and violent messages throughout our culture. Overexposure to violent images is desensitizing us to violence. Because it now takes more and more violence to make us feel shock and revulsion, media violence has to become more and more graphic to be profitable. We are addicted—and we're about to overdose.

These disturbing messages are also reaching a larger and younger audience. The technological revolution has created home videocassette recorders, cable television, music videos, movie rental cassettes, compact discs, and satellite dishes providing a myriad of choices in home entertainment. Never before have such high-powered and diverse media been available to so many people, including the very youngest children. But these new marvels have a darker side. They can enhance educational and cultural opportunities—or they can spread new forms of graphic violence.

Parents should closely examine the smorgasbord of violent entertainment now offered to our children. The spread of simulated violence should be evaluated against the backdrop of steadily increasing violence in real life.

HEAVY METAL: THROBBING CHORDS AND VIOLENT LYRICS

Heavy metal and its loyal fan following represent a new phenomenon in rock music. Focusing on the darker, violent side of life, this brand of music was first played in England some twenty years ago as a vehicle for countercultural rebellion. Many of the songs were political. But the frustration and rebellion that is a normal part of the maturation process for many young people who are critical of adults and "the Establishment" seemed to turn to greater and greater despair. The music took an even darker turn and explored subjects like devil worship and the occult, sadistic sex, murder, rape, and suicide.

Defenders of such songs say that these things are occurring in the real world, that they are moving to the forefront of our consciousness, and that therefore the music should be seen as simply an artistic reflection of new realities. Others argue that emphasizing these themes in pop culture will in itself push them into the popular mind.

Perhaps the youth of the eighties have to go to new extremes such as these to get their parents' attention.

It must be hard to rebel against a generation of adults who have broken quite a few taboos themselves.

The names of some of these bands imply a fascination with violence and evil: Venom, the Dead Kennedys, Suicidal Tendencies, W.A.S.P. (which, according to them, stands for "We Are Sexual Perverts"[2]), Judas Priest, Iron Maiden, Warlord, Metallica, Predator, the Scorpions, Slayer, and Black Sabbath. Certain of these heavy metal and punk rock bands make violence (particularly sexual violence), explicit sex, and the power of evil central themes in their concert performances and recordings.

Heavy metal does not yet receive a lot of Top Forty radio airplay, and MTV has reportedly cut back on the airing of some of their videos, although they do broadcast a heavy metal hour. But heavy metal songs are played regularly on many radio stations and college campuses, and heavy metal videocassette sales are surprisingly strong.

Most of the heavy metal bands record for small independent labels and will "only" sell perhaps 250,000 to 400,000 copies. These groups tour the country and can build up substantial numbers of fans by playing live concerts and selling their records by mail order. Increasingly, those independent labels are being distributed by the six major corporate record labels. This is a business decision which will further promote heavy metal to the public.

In concert, the most strident bands not only play their music at the highest decibels, but perform what they describe as "vaudeville acts" that glamorize explicit sex, alcohol and drug use, and bloody violence. Some depict the most extreme antisocial behavior imaginable. *Most* of their fans are adolescent boys between the ages of twelve and nineteen, although recently girls have made up a greater percentage of the audience. Some fans are younger still—aged eight, nine, and ten.

A male rock star, Alice Cooper, was one of the early proponents of "shock rock." He used props like guillotines and giant boa constrictor snakes to terrify and excite the audience. The band Kiss elaborated on Cooper's theatrical violence and drew nationwide protests and devoted fans. They were the first to use grotesque makeup and outrageous costumes. In England, Ozzy Osbourne, long-time lead vocalist for the heavy metal band Black Sabbath, horrified rock enthusiasts by biting off the head of a live bat during one frenzied performance. Heavy metal headliners are now competing with each other to be the most outrageous and socially unacceptable, which seems to assure them instant success among young fans.

PUSHING THE LIMITS

W.A.S.P. released an album of the same name that was replete with songs about death and sex. It included lyrics such as "Sex and pain the same,/ They're really the same."[3] The band's lead singer has convulsed audiences by throwing raw meat into the crowd. The band has also used skeletons, axes, blades, and gallons of fake blood as props. To promote their act, they have used a picture of a bloodied, half-naked woman chained to a torture rack. Past performances have included the simulated attack and torture of a woman. Reportedly, in the act lead singer Blackie Lawless wore between his legs a codpiece adorned with a circular saw blade. He pretended to beat a woman who was naked except for a G-string and a black hood over her head, and as fake blood cascaded from under the hood, he seemed to attack her with the blade.[4] In another version of the act, he pretended to slit her throat. As Adrianne Stone reports in the January 1985 edition of *Hit Parader*, "[W.A.S.P. are] the deranged demons who bind a loincloth-clad female onto a 'rack,' then 'slit' her neck until she shakes and convulses into oblivion."[5]

The cover of the W.A.S.P. twelve-inch single record *F**k Like a Beast* shows a close-up of a man holding his bloody hands on his thighs, with a bloody circular saw blade protruding from his genital area.[6] Although imported from England, this album was for sale in record stores throughout the U.S.

In an October 1985 article in the fan magazine *Hit Parader*, which advertised the band through a cover photograph of Blackie Lawless, blood running out of his mouth, holding up a bloody skull, the singer talked about his heavy metal exploits:

> To me rock is theater, electric vaudeville. . . . It's the place where you can do just about anything and get away with it. It's a zone where rules and restrictions are just totally thrown out the window. It's like controlled anarchy—if there is such a thing. We spit blood and throw raw pieces of meat into the crowd. We're not trying to make any great social statement;

we're just trying to entertain and give the people who come to see us a good time.[7]

Thank goodness they're not interested in social statements. Not only does this package appeal to some children, it appealed to Capitol Records, who must have seen W.A.S.P. as just the band to promote to the nation's youth. The group signed a $1.5 million record deal with Capitol.[8]

Rock music fan magazines freely publicize this violent, gruesome entertainment, gleefully reporting and dramatizing the "fun." In September 1985 *Faces Rocks* carried a story about the "hot 'n' nasty" W.A.S.P. band. Band member Lawless told writer Keith Greenberg that "nastiness" is central to the W.A.S.P. performance. "I don't mean vulgar 'nasty,' " he said. "I mean violent. We sound like a tin can ripped open with your hands, that kind of nasty. It doesn't leave a clean cut."[9] Anger helps fuel the violence Blackie Lawless and other heavy metal rockers inject into their performances. "The anger is what helps you relate to the kids," he said in the same interview. "When you got adolescents and you put in a healthy dose of hostility, you got a lethal combination there. That's what makes rock 'n' roll what it is. You're pissed off. *I'm* still pissed off about a lot of things; thank God I haven't lost that. I think the worst thing that can happen to any rock 'n' roller is getting civilized."[10] Well, maybe rock doesn't have to get civilized in a middle-class sense, but it doesn't have to promote barbarism either.

Parents should listen closely to the messages in heavy metal. A song by the popular Mötley Crüe offers this view of a romantic interlude:

> I'll either break her face
> Or take down her legs,
> Get my ways at will.
> Go for the throat,
> Never let loose,
> Going in for the kill.[11]

Or consider this from their two million seller: "Out go the lights/In goes my knife/Pull out his life/Consider that bastard dead."[12]

Some youngsters will get hold of a 1986 album called *Carnivore*, by a band with the same name, and will listen to the sickening lyrics of "Predator":

> I sense that living human beings dwell below my feet
> an important source of protein you are what you eat
>
> . . . .
>
> broken splintered bones, boiling blood
> torn and bleeding skin
> blackened burning flesh melting fat
> amputated limbs
> eviscerated, lungs torn out
> heart ripped from the chest
> decapitated, a meal of vaginas and breasts.[13]

Some heavy metal songs extol the virtues of torture, rape, and murder of women. They usually portray women as sexual playthings and as victims—objects of pleasure designed, like alcohol and drugs or fast cars, for men to use and abuse. Many of the album covers of heavy metal groups present glimpses of this anger-spurred violence.

The cover of Exciter's album *Violence & Force* depicts a homicidal attack; as a woman's hands desperately try to hold shut a door, a killer has thrust both hands, one holding a dagger, the other dripping blood, through the open crack.[14] Abattoir's *Vicious Attack* shows a woman's torso with a man's arms wrapped around her from behind. In one hand the man holds a dagger, in the other a sharpened meathook which he presses to the woman's breast.[15] The album *Savage Grace* boasts a color photograph of a nude woman gagged and chained to a motorcycle,[16] and the album *Be My Slave* shows a scantily clad woman on her knees, holding sadomasochistic tools of the trade in her hands.[17]

This kind of message is spilling over into the musical mainstream. The cover of the album *Undercover*, by the Rolling Stones (not a heavy metal band), shows a nude woman lying on her back with a triangle placed over her pubic area. One song on the album is entitled "Tie You Up (The Pain of Love)."[18]

Children are also portrayed as victims of brutal violence by some of these bands. One group, tastelessly styled the Dead Kennedys, has a song called "I Kill Children." It goes like this: "I kill children,/I love to see them die./I kill children,/I make their mothers cry."[19] Another band, Slayer, known for its dedicated satanic lyrics, sings in a song entitled "Kill Again": "Kill the preacher's only son/Watch the infant die/Bodily dismemberment/Drink the purest blood."[20]

DOES IT REALLY MATTER?

Is all this just entertainment? A 1986 study by two professors at California State University at Fullerton concluded that teens don't listen to the words of songs, just to the beat. The researchers contend that parents hear more sophisticated themes in the songs than the children really understand.[21] However, common sense and virtually every other study on the topic suggest otherwise.

The healthy, mature personality may in fact be minimally affected by violent messages. But for many malleable teens and preteens who are searching for identity and who are beset by conflicts about authority, drugs, sex, religion, and education, a big dose of heavy metal messages like these can be extremely harmful.

Dr. Joseph Stuessy, professor of music at the University of Texas at San Antonio and author of *The Heavy Metal User's Manual,* holds that music *does* affect behavior. "Any kind of music affects our moods, emotions, attitudes and our resultant behavior," he says. "Music has both psychological and physiological effects on people. That's why we have choirs and organs in churches and synagogues, bands at football games, Muzak in business and doctors' offices, military marches, background music for movies and television programs, Jazzercise where legions of people are motivated to move by rock music, and most important, commercial jingles."[22]

Plato wrote that music had the power to shape society. Today, those who orchestrate the successful commercial jingle can certainly control social and commercial behavior. Advertisers would not spend billions annually if music and other messages were not persuasive. According to Dr. Stuessy, music aids retention of verbal messages; we are more likely to remember a message if it comes to us in a musical context. Repetition makes us more likely to internalize—and like—a message. The more senses the message involves—like sight, hearing, or touch—the more likely that message will have an impact on our conscious and subconscious minds. Dr. Stuessy warns that heavy metal music differs categorically from earlier forms of popular music and from mainstream rock and roll. With its celebration of extreme violence, substance abuse, explicit sex, and satanism, one of heavy metal's main themes is hatred. "I know personally of no form of popular music before which has had hatred as one of its central themes," he says.[23]

As radio consultant Lee Abrams allegedly stated, heavy metal may be "the music to kill your parents by."[24] Teens who listen to heavy metal get that message of hate overtly or covertly. I've received many letters from teens who like heavy metal and who say, in effect, "Hey, I'm not gonna go out and kill someone just because that is in the lyrics." But while they will not go to that extreme, Dr. Stuessy points out that "anyone who says, 'I can listen to heavy metal, but it doesn't affect me,' is simply wrong. It simply affects different people in different degrees and different ways."[25]

Another rock and roll expert cites examples of teen homicides, suicides, and other violent acts linked to a youth's involvement with, among other things, heavy metal music. Dr. Paul King, medical director of the adolescent program at Charter Lakeside Hospital, a psychiatric and addictive disease facility in Memphis, Tennessee, says that over 80 percent of the adolescent patients he treats have listened to heavy metal music for several hours a day. Dr. King notes that over 50 percent of them know the words to the songs and can write them down. A number of students spend school time writing and memorizing the words, he adds; "the lyrics become a philosophy of life, a religion."[26]

Since we began the Parents' Music Resource Center, we have read many letters and reports indicating that the messages of violent hatred in the "religion" of heavy metal do influence and help corrupt; in some extreme cases, they even seem to play a part in ending young lives. Undoubtedly, there are other important factors in all these cases, but the messages of the music can be regarded, at the very least, as a symptom of some distress, if the young person is troubled. If more people understood that, they might be able to intervene and help the young person.

One such letter came from a mother in San Antonio, Texas. She has experienced a tragedy that she feels is directly related to the influence of music on behavior. This woman told me that in the summer of 1980, her sixteen-year-old son went into a trancelike state on a very hot summer night. He was listening to Pink Floyd's album *The Wall*. He had not been able to sleep because his allergies were acting up, and he had a severe headache. His aunt was asleep on the couch in front of the TV set, which was beaming a violent episode of "Starsky and Hutch" about a serial killer of prostitutes. The boy suddenly stabbed his aunt to death. He claims not even to remember the act.

According to the police report, there were no drugs involved, just the hot weather, the headache, the TV, and the music. Her son "believes the music itself can hypnotize you," she says. At this writing her son is now in prison, and she and her family have exhausted all means of appealing the case.

There are many other recent cases of children committing similar types of murders. In May 1986, the *Tacoma News Tribune* reported that a twenty-year-old boy murdered his mother with an ax and a pair of scissors, in the course of raping her. He was ruled sane for trial; the defense plans to plead that the influence of satanism and heavy metal music caused the boy to commit these acts.[27] To date, however, no such defense has been successful in the courts.

We should be deeply concerned about the obvious cumulative effect of this cult of violence that has captured the public's imagination and pervaded our society. Few parents realize how much the angry brand of music that is part of it has presented suicide, glorified rape, and condoned murder. The message is more than repulsive—it's deadly.

TELEVISION PROGRAMMING, VIDEO-CASSETTE RECORDERS AND MUSIC VIDEOS

TELEVISION

Television is the most accessible entertainment medium of all, with 98 percent of American households owning at least one set. Cable television now reaches some thirty-eight million homes; another two million households own satellite dishes.

The levels of violence on television have dramatically changed for the worse over the last five years. We now view movies on television replete with graphic, sickening violence. Remember the reports of people getting sick and fainting while watching *The Exorcist* in the movie house, back in 1974? Some television stations now show this movie in the early evening, when children could be watching. One television station, KCOP in Los Angeles, began a "Clint Eastwood Festival" showing extremely violent movies such as *Fist Full of Dollars* in early prime time on weeknights. A viewer reported that the festival was promoted on at least one occasion with a graphic murder scene excerpted from one of the movies in a commercial break during a Saturday morning cartoon show. A man in Nashville wrote me about how outraged he was to see *Straw Dogs*—a movie that contains a graphic rape scene—on his television set in the middle of an afternoon. I have heard many other parents complain about gratuitous violence that has scared the wits out of their child. They are the ones who have to soothe the children and banish the nightmares.

Television is a subtle teacher, welcomed into every home. Perhaps we need to step back from it to examine more critically some of the images that penetrate our consciousness from our new electronic hearth. If there is any doubt that television has a powerful influence, consider that its primary purpose is to sell products, and that advertisements certainly influence behavior. Ironically, some of the same television executives who make a living selling ads try to suggest that the medium does not influence behavior.

I have been concerned about violence on television and its effects on children for several years. In 1977 I helped form a group of congressional wives who joined a coalition with the National PTA, the American Academy of Pediatrics, and approximately thirty other groups. This coalition went to the networks to express concern about televised violence. During this activity, I met Ann Kahn, who would later become national president of the PTA, and talked with her about the most recent outcry from the religious, academic, and medical communities over the growing levels of violence on television. I asked her if this barrage of fictionalized violence in our homes was numbing us to the real horror of violence. Was it making violent behavior more acceptable?

Ann Kahn has known for some time that there is a grass-roots answer to those crucial questions. America's teachers have been warning about the effects of television violence for years, she told me:

> Now studies are legitimizing our case that was made eight years ago. Teachers noticed that children were more violent. They observed that child's play had become more violent and aggressive and that children seemed less sensitive to the pain that is a part of violence. Finally, after eight years, our trying to say that this is a legitimate concern not only for children, but for adults because it desensitizes them to violence, is gaining acceptance. Back then, everyone laughed about it and pooh-poohed it.

We were concerned then about the long-range implications of becoming desensitized [to violence]. Now we have a generation of kids grown up accepting violence and we're paying the price for that—all of us, whether we've got children or not. It becomes a moral issue—whether or not our nation is going to accept violence as an acceptable way of life.

The problem is a grave one because what we are telling our children is that violence is an acceptable kind of behavior in solving problems. Now we are having problems with youth forming gangs—the violence is so glamorized. Another problem is that the violence is so gratuitous—violence that is not necessary for the plot, is so insidious. It is not natural violence, but violence thrown in to shock and titillate. There's the evil in that problem and the kids accept it as a normal way of life. If they've been raised with a lot of TV, they have no other frame of reference, so it seems normal to solve problems with violence. If you don't like what someone said, just run over them in a car, or beat them up. We are seeing some very frightening results. We are seeing young adults saying violence is a way of life.

As access to televised violence increases, what can we do? Mrs. Kahn acknowledged the difficulty of keeping family control. "Practically everyone has a VCR, and it is increasingly difficult to control what children see. Cable television provides more choice, and I think that in some respect this is healthy and has allowed a great variety of programming. But along with that are shows that appeal to the worst instincts in people and these are widely available and accessible." She reflected about the battles with the network executives: "I see little hope of them taking any significant action, particularly in the face of public apathy. But I'm not so sure the public is going to continue to be apathetic." Mrs. Kahn continued:

> The reality within the broadcast community is rooted in a pure market ethic; if it sells, it must be okay. Violence on TV is commercially successful. If no one liked it, no one would watch it and advertisers wouldn't pay for it. That's what the networks will tell you. I think that is a pretty low standard to use. I remember in some of our PTA hearings on television violence, a woman and a network executive were exchanging views. He said that the public shouldn't be concerned with the content of television, and asked networks to exercise more self-restraint, because all the parent has to do is know the location of the "off" button. And she replied: "You're asking me to turn off the faucet and ignore the fact that you continue to poison the water." Obviously, both have obligations. And now, with everyone at work and fewer adults in the home to push the off button, this new social reality increases the responsibility of the industry. The parents can set standards for their own children, but it's also incumbent on the industry to be more responsible.

The industry, in the past, has ridiculed the idea of its being some kind of "national nanny." It will take enormous public pressure to force change. As Mrs. Kahn put it, "They must first recognize what they are doing to our national life."

"I think the violence will get a lot worse," Mrs. Kahn observed. "And I am afraid that will eventually push some objectors to take measures that go beyond the Constitution. We all accept freedom of expression, but there is a big step beyond that to a total lack of standards or self-restraint."

More and more researchers are succeeding in measuring the link between television violence and individual behavior. By the time a student graduates high school, he or she will have seen eighteen thousand murders on television. With the appearance of such action series as "Hunter" and "Miami Vice," television violence continues to increase.

Dr. George Gerbner of the Annenberg School of Communications at the University of Pennsylvania released a study on television violence in September 1986. The new study concluded that the nation's children are bombarded with more family-hour television violence than at any time since 1967.[28]

"For the first time in our experience," Dr. Gerbner explained to a reporter, "the early evening television hour, when the largest number of children are in the viewing audience, is now the most violent hour on network television." The study showed that women were more likely than men to end up as the victims rather than the victors in violent encounters. The researchers also found that weekend daytime entertainment was substantially more violent than network prime-time programming. "This shows a reckless disregard for . . . the welfare of our children," said Gerbner. He added that television violence numbs viewers to real violence and makes them more fearful of the real world.[29]

Dr. Gerbner's views on televised violence are illuminating. That the violence is seen as "entertaining" helps it go down smoothly, he says. "There is no pain, no gore, no consequences of the violent action. Therein lies the more insidious lesson of televised violence. When the violence is sugar coated, it is more deadly." Dr. Gerbner also observes that violence has changed over the years:

> The approach on a show like "The A-Team," for example, which uses a variety of military weapons without anyone ever actually getting killed, presents the problem of uninterrupted sequences of sanitized, yet action-oriented violence as a solution to almost any problem.

Dr. Gerbner also raises another question. Why is there so much violence directed against those most vulnerable in our society? He offers the following analysis:

> The violence demonstrates power. Its message is: Who can get away with doing what to whom. And this is a powerful, insidious message to learn. The violence teaches that the powerless people are easy to intimidate—the women, children and the elderly. The real danger is that this continues the inequities and injustice that is ingrained in our society. I am more concerned about this aspect than explicit brutality—it's pathological to get a kick or charge out of that. The unequal power relations of these shows cause people thus portrayed to see themselves as more likely to be victimized in real life.[30]

But times are changing. The public is more receptive to critics of television violence and more energetic in complaining about it than it's been in a long time. The industry is becoming worried that it is vulnerable to harsher legislation. Some people in the networks are moving to protect themselves by restoring the National Association of Broadcasters code of standards. The federal government had forced the networks to dismantle the one standard that they all subscribed to, arguing that it violated antitrust laws. It was a misguided action, to be sure. But the code may be resurrected, thanks to legislation being pushed by Senator Paul Simon of Illinois.

"There is a renewed commitment in the direction of simply paying attention to television and its effects," said Dr. Gerbner. He calls on parents, educators, and religious and community leaders to join in a new environmental movement. This movement would mobilize citizens concerned with the degradation of the physical environment to also turn their attention to the cultural environment.[31] Action for Children's Television, a nonprofit child advocacy organization, is working to improve children's television by encouraging diversity in programming, discouraging the overcommercialization of such programming, and eliminating deceptive commercials for children.

Children watch an astounding average of thirty hours of television a week. Child care experts say that one or two hours a day of carefully chosen programs is the most they should see. The National PTA, pediatricians, health care professionals, and other experts are trying to make people recognize that all this violence is not benign. Television is shaping the hearts and minds and attitudes of an entire generation of children who—like their parents—are turned on to this plug-in drug.

Network executives offer this fare because it nets the biggest return for their dollar. They seem to have completely forgotten their responsibility to the public trust. According to the Federal Communication Act of 1934, commercial station operators, as public trustees, have a legal obligation to serve children. But aside from a decent show or two, they offer a steady diet of action-packed violence. Moreover, the broadcasting trade magazines read by television station managers often feature ads encouraging them to buy violent programs to increase their ratings. One movie syndication company puts it this way: "Pull in the big ratings of teen and adult viewers with . . . sixteen exploitation films. . . . Take your viewers beyond the edge of their seats and to the brink of madness."[32] Another says: "So if you want to get tough in the ratings . . . call . . . and ask for our Hell on Reels. And wreak havoc on an unsuspecting population."[33]

And of course, it's likely to get even worse. That is the trend. For example, *Broadcasting* magazine reported that Paramount plans to develop a television series based on *Friday the 13th*, making the teen killer thriller available to all children.[34] No doubt the stores will stock little "Jason" toys, complete with tiny hockey masks.

VIDEOCASSETTE RECORDERS—CANDY ON THE SHELF

Viewers now have another means to expand their entertainment possibilities—the videocassette recorder (VCR). VCR owners have access to an incredible variety of fine material. But on the same shelves are an increasing number of atrocious horror films, crammed with grisly, graphic violence, which viewers can select for home entertainment kicks.

Nationwide, video stores will rent any kind of show desired, including such favorites as *Faces of Death,* which portrays real (and gruesome) deaths; *The Texas Chainsaw Massacre,* providing bodies sliced up with power tools; *I Spit on Your Grave,* highlighting the bloody revenge of a raped woman; *2000 Maniacs,* in which a southern hamlet doubles as a torture chamber and human slaughterhouse; and *Splatter University,* which needs no further description.

How many parents are aware of the growing popularity among teens of slasher films? Their subjects are not much different from heavy metal themes, and they are often even more graphic, searing powerful visual images into the young brain.

Here's how one observer described a scene from a recent horror movie: "Several men hold an attractive woman on a pool table. She is screaming, struggling. Her terror increases when one of the men appears with an ax. He swings—and cleanly severs her arm at the shoulder—as other persons clap and shout. The men take the woman's arm—leaving her in shock on the table—and proceed to barbecue it on an outdoor grill."[35]

This depraved scene is on *Terror on Tape,* a popular videocassette that is an anthology of scenes of sexual violence against women, culled from horror movies. *Filmgore* is a similar compilation of scenes from slasher movies. *Filmgore's* promotional copy reads: "See blood-thirsty, butcher killer[s] . . . and sadistic slayers slash, strangle, mangle and mutilate bare-breasted beauties in bondage."[36]

Many of these films involve scenes of sexual

violence that should earn them an X rating or restrict them to the under-the-counter porn trade. These kinds of tapes are bought and rented primarily by teens and are readily available without restrictions in neighborhood video stores. In many cases, they are not rated, or if they are, the rating is not enforced.

Because movies now include record levels of violence, the National Coalition on Television Violence (NCTV), premier watchdog and research organization on the subject, turned its monitoring spotlight to new movies produced for the summer of 1986. It listed Sylvester Stallone, Arnold Schwarzenegger, Charles Bronson, and Chuck Norris as the most violent actors, and Cannon Films, which produced or distributed seven of the ten most violent films, as the worst offending distributor.[37]

Now, of course, the appetite for explicit violence is growing. *Texas Chainsaw Massacre: Part 2*, now available as a home video, for example, offers graphic, hideous blood, terror, and torture as campy entertainment. It includes the skinning of a person. And it is not rated.

THE MUSIC VIDEO—NEW KID ON THE TUBE

Violent music videos can have a similar impact on younger children. MTV, the twenty-four-hour rock music television channel which has become one of the most important promotional media for new songs, provides this visual expansion. Many of the videos it airs actually reinforce or even exceed the violence and sexual explicitness of other television shows.

In an analysis of music videos, Professors Barry L.

Sherman and Joseph R. Dominick of the University of Georgia concluded that videos are "violent, male-oriented, and laden with sexual content." In fairness, it should be noted that 56 percent of music videos were analyzed as containing violence versus 75 percent of all prime-time television.[38]

Dr. George Gerbner has said that "it's not that violence is so popular with the viewers, it's just that it's cheap to produce." The NCTV also found that more than half of the videos on MTV feature violence. In its 1984 report, NCTV provided several examples of violent videos:

• Mötley Crüe's *Looks That Kill* involves women in cages being attacked by the studded-leather–clad male band. A laser-shooting woman frees them and sets the band on fire.

• Billy Idol's *Dancing with Myself* shows the star using electricity to blow people off a building. A man sharpens a straight-edge razor as if to kill a naked woman, in chains behind a translucent sheet. A man with a hammer sneaks up on a woman to kill her.

• *Torture* by the Jacksons features a woman with extremely long nails and shackled wrists. Women in cages claw at the singer, who falls into a web guarded by a woman with a whip; the woman whips a skeleton.

• Def Leppard's *Fooling* shows an eyeless woman playing a harp, a man in bondage tortured three times by a woman, and skulls on fire.[39]

How does a four- or six-year-old react to some of these quick little snippets of video? They make up a big part of the audience. A teen may only pick up subtle messages about the role of women and the enormous value placed on sexiness. But these images may terrify the younger child. A visual image doesn't have to be on the screen for very long to have an impact. My six-year-old was disturbed by Tom Petty's *Don't Come Around Here No More* because the last scene showed an Alice (of Wonderland fame) turning into a cake and being sliced up. We adults must not forget, in our desensitized state, the effects these images have on children of all ages.

Some music videos, while violent, do have an educational intent, NCTV noted. For instance, in *Beat It*, Michael Jackson gets warring gangs to lay down their chains, clubs, and switchblades and dance with him. Aldo Nova's *Monkey on Your Back* puts down drug abuse as dangerous. NCTV also praised five groups or singers whose videos feature primarily pro-social themes: U-2; Julian Lennon; the Romantics; Donna Summer; and Missing Persons.

In spite of such positive dramatizations and some effort by cable channel management to reject music videos that "go beyond the bounds of good taste," MTV still presents a heavily violent diet to its young watchers. "The message is that violence is normal and OK," according to Dr. Thomas Radecki, NCTV chairman and psychiatrist on the staff of the University of Illinois School of Medicine, "that hostile sexual relations between men and women are common and acceptable, that heroes actively engage in torture and murders of others for fun."[40]

THE HARM OF VIDEO VIOLENCE

Media images mirror and shape society, reflecting trends and realities, but also validating and reinforcing them. Many tend to remain unconcerned about media violence, accepting it simply because it imitates and dramatizes the violence in society and the world. Some are not convinced of its harm. Some go so far as to suggest, as do the violent heavy metal rockers, that exaggerated, fictionalized violence in movies, television, and music videos even has a cathartic value, allowing viewers to purge themselves of their own base instincts. While this may be true for some, the evidence with respect to most people suggests otherwise.

• Dr. Milton Eisenhower headed the National Commission on the Causes and Prevention of Violence, which reported back in 1969 that "violence on television encourages violent forms of behavior and fosters moral and social values about violence in daily life which are unacceptable in civilized society." The commission urged broadcasters to reduce overall levels of violence in programs, take the violence out of children's cartoons, and schedule crime, western, and adventure stories containing violence after 9:00 P.M.[41] But broadcasters didn't do this, and the violence got worse.

• In March 1972, the surgeon general of the United States, Dr. Jesse Steinfeld, told the Senate Subcommittee on Communications: "It is clear to me that the causal relationship between televised violence and antisocial behavior is sufficient to warrant appropriate and immediate remedial action. The data on social phenomena such as television and/or aggressive behavior will never be clear enough for all social scientists to agree on the formulation of a succinct statement of causality. But there comes a time when the data are sufficient to justify action. That time has come."[42]

● Professor Neil Malamuth, chairman of communications studies at the University of California at Los Angeles, and Professor Edward Donnerstein, a psychologist at the Center for Communications Research at the University of Wisconsin, have both conducted studies that suggest viewers of media violence are detrimentally affected. Their research has shown that watching a steady diet of graphic sexual violence has caused some men to accept the idea that violence against women, such as rape, is acceptable.[43]

Professor Donnerstein uses the terms *aggressive pornography* and *sexually violent media images* to emphasize that "it is the violent images in pornography that account for the various research effects." He emphasizes that other research over the past decade has demonstrated that nonviolent sexual images do not stimulate aggressive behavior, rape, or antisocial behavior. However, the professor reports that research in laboratory settings "has shown that male subjects act more aggressively against women after exposure to violent forms of pornography."[44]

● Dr. David Pearl of the National Institute of Mental Health carried out a study demonstrating that television violence does affect violent behavior. He reports on four identified effects of television violence on viewers: (1) It provides how-to-do-it training for viewers inclined to imitate observed behavior; (2) it can trigger violence that the viewer

73

might have otherwise repressed; (3) it desensitizes viewers to the occurrence of violence; (4) it increases viewer fearfulness.[45]

• Dr. George Comstock of Syracuse University found more than one hundred significant research projects that positively correlate media violence and aggressiveness.[46]

• In September 1985, the National Council of the Churches of Christ in the U.S.A. (National Council of Churches) released a significant report that was very strongly stated. The report concluded: "Violence and sexual violence must be reduced in the media. We believe this goal can be attained, without depriving those in the media of the means of livelihood or of the rewards which are justly theirs, and without depriving citizens of their First Amendment guarantee of freedom of speech."[47]

• In 1985, the Council of Representatives of the American Psychological Association adopted a resolution citing potential dangers in television violence and concluding that a link exists between violence on children's programs and aggressive behavior in children. This is exactly what the nation's teachers were saying in the 1978 hearings of the National PTA. A resolution of the PTA encouraged parents to supervise children's television viewing; it also asked the television industry to reduce the violence in children's fiction programs, which children might imitate, and further urged more research on lessening the impact of television violence on children.[48] These measures may have been in part a response to the death of a young child who hanged himself in imitation of a "Scooby-Doo" cartoon character that had hanged himself. The child was four years old.[49] NCTV turned up a number of research projects that document the harmful effects of violent music video entertainment. Dr. Susan Reilly and Dr. Sharas Rehman of the University of Miami in Oxford, Ohio, stated in their study of violent music videos "that students became somewhat more desensitized to violence after viewing only five violent videos." Later Dr. Rehman completed a similar study of over one hundred college students at Pennsylvania State University and found similar results.[50]

While he notes that music video violence is not necessarily more violent than that seen on prime-time television, Dr. Radecki emphasizes the need to consider four "key factors" when dealing with violent music videos:

1. Studies by the U.S. surgeon general, the expert panel of the National Institute of Mental Health, the U.S. Department of Justice, and the U.S. Attorney General's Task Force on Family Violence have all provided "overwhelming evidence that violence on prime-time television has important harmful effects on normal children and adult viewers."
2. Music videos appeal to adolescents and preadolescents who have less ability to understand the potentially harmful effects of violent entertainment.
3. Music videos include more violence between the sexes and more sadistic violence than in

the violence depicted on prime-time television.

4. Viewers have no choice of music videos on MTV; they may at any time during their viewing suddenly confront "unexpected images of violence, sadism and callous sexual portrayals."

"Despite overwhelming evidence of harm," Dr. Radecki indicates, "there are no warnings of harm, and no non-violent, non-degrading alternatives in rock music video entertainment."[51]

At the time that NCTV released its music video report, Dr. Radecki expressed concern about the "growing culture of violence" in rock music. Drawing on his experiences as a psychiatrist, he stated:

> I have already seen several cases of young people in my psychiatric practice with severe problems of anger and anti-social behavior who are deeply immersed into a subculture of violent rock music. They each own several dozen tee-shirts with violent images of various heavy metal groups on them and wear various types of metal-studded jewelry and barbed-wire necklaces. It is plainly obvious that they are heavily immersed in fantasies of violence that also are affecting their way of thinking and their behavior in an anti-social direction.[52]

PARENTS' CALL TO ACTION

How can you help your child make the right choices about violent messages, whether in music or on television? Let's take them one by one.

1. Get involved with your child. Talk about the music he or she likes. Concentrate on the content, even if you don't like the musical style. By listening to the music with your child, you are giving him or her the important message that you care.
2. Help your child make musical choices that are positive. Go with him or her to the record store, examine the albums, discuss the groups. Do this in an open, supportive, communicative manner. Give guidance. This applies equally to younger children and adolescents.
3. Talk about popular groups with your children. Listen to their likes and dislikes. Teach them that they don't have to patronize musical groups that exploit women and commercialize violence. Point out that it does matter when someone buys an album or tape by a group that is exploitative.
4. If your child is exclusively preoccupied with heavy metal music, you may want to get more involved and find out why. Heavy metal dwells on destructive, violent, nihilistic themes. Too many parents have written letters to the PMRC expressing dismay over the fact that they didn't know what this music represented for their child until it was too late. It *can* be a warning signal. Untroubled youth also may like heavy metal and be entirely unaffected. All parents must judge for themselves.
5. Talk with your child about how one's choice

of music is a barometer of mental health. Joe Stuessy points out that kids need to be as aware and conscious of their mental diet as they are of their physical diet, because both contribute to their sense of well-being. Opting for a diet of heavy metal music means you are ingesting graphic messages about hatred, murder, suicide, sadomasochism, satanism, and just generally depressing and negative themes. "Try moving away from heavy metal to normal rock and roll," he suggests.[53]

6. Go with your child to concerts. I realize that older teens would rather clean up their rooms than be seen with you at a concert, so just go by yourself to see what goes on there.

You can help your child decide what kinds of television shows to watch, too. As role models, parents will be the ones to teach them (and to make sure they don't watch too much).

1. Do not leave the television set on all the time. This encourages indiscriminate viewing.

2. The television should be used to see a show for a certain reason, and then shut off.

3. Parents should view television shows with their children as often as possible. Sit down and watch with them. They will appreciate the shared time, as well as discussing the program with you. You will find out what's being aired.

4. Make a list of approved programs. If the child

resists, cut back the rights to watch them.

5. Some child care specialists feel that about one hour a day is all that younger children should watch. Consider adopting that rule.

6. Television watching can sneak up on you. Tune into your child's viewing habits if you haven't been aware of them and decide if you think your child is watching too much. If so, cut back.

7. Don't let television crowd out other good experiences, like reading, game playing, or family activities.

8. VCRs can offer the choice of quality viewing, if that is what you provide. Buy, rent, or tape movies, specials, or educational programs. Set firm rules about violent and pornographic movies.

9. Give your child guidelines about movies he or she can see. Most important, let them know *why*.

Selling More Than the Sizzle: Explicit Sex in the Media

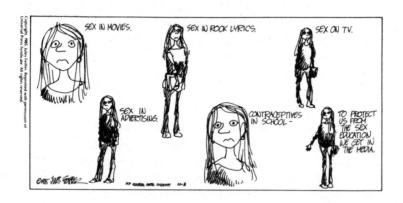

Sexuality has always been a major theme in music. In fact, "rock and roll" was once slang for sexual intercourse. But the depersonalization, commercialization, and trivialization of sex, driven in part by public acceptance of soft-core pornography in such men's magazines as *Playboy* and *Penthouse,* have succeeded in separating sex from emotional involvement and commitment. At the same time, the engines of hard-core porn have created an enormous, multibillion-dollar appetite in America. More than ever before, sex is for sale in the media. The commercialization of sex has pervaded our society.

We have exploited the good gift of sex, and cheapened human dignity in the process.

LYRICS TO LURE

As singer Smokey Robinson, rock performer Sting, and others have noted, this trend toward more explicit sexual themes has now spread to popular music aimed at young children and teens, music that plays a significant role in the lives of young people. Teenagers' idols can have a major impact on their attitudes and values. Many popular music idols of the young now sing about rape, masturbation, incest, bondage, violence, and just plain intercourse. This "auditory pornography," as Smokey Robinson calls it, has become a tempting appetizer on the abundant menu of pornography offered in the United States— one that is being fed to younger and younger audiences.

Responsible parents object to the notion that their children should be introduced to the subjects of masturbation, intercourse, or sexual sadism by singers like Prince and Sheena Easton or groups like Mötley Crüe and W.A.S.P. It's important for parents to discuss such topics with their children, but parents have the responsibility and right to set the agenda and context of the discussion themselves.

No one wants to take sex out of music, but the amount of explicit descriptions of sex currently being marketed to youngsters must be reconsidered. Unhappily, some artists prostitute sexual themes for their own commercial gain, while exacting a heavy price from our children in the process.

It is a quantum leap from the Beatles' "I Want to Hold Your Hand" to Prince singing: "If you get tired of masturbating. . ./If you like, I'll jack you off."[1] It's a long way from the Rolling Stones' "Let's Spend the Night Together," which drew protests in its day, to Sheena Easton's "Sugar Walls": "You can't fight passion when passion is hot/Temperatures rise inside my sugar walls."[2] Where Elvis sang "Little Sister" about his attraction to his girlfriend's younger sister, Prince now sings "Sister": "My sister never made love/To anyone else but me. . . ./Incest is everything it's said to be."[3]

Even the most tolerant and liberal among us are tested by these developments in the public domain. Attitudes toward sexuality are a matter of private and individual taste. Liberal attitudes are traditionally very tolerant of a wide variety of private sexual practices and expressions. But even the most tolerant laws have always applied different criteria to the detailed, explicit expression of private sexual acts in public, especially when young children are in the audience.

So what are we to think of "Nasty Girl" by Vanity, another Prince protegé, who sings throatily, "I want seven inches or more";[4] or Ted Nugent's "Wango Tango" which goes like this: "When I need some lubrication, baby,/You get a belly propped down,/You get a butt propped up,/Yeah . . . I think you're in the right position, baby."[5]

Consider these lines from "Relax," by the band Frankie Goes to Hollywood: "Relax, don't do it,/When you want to suck or chew it,/Relax, don't do it,/When you want to come."[6] Or these, from "Ouch," by Vanity:

> When you kiss me, when you love me
> Oooh—you make me cream
> It hurts so good, I just got to scream
> . . . .
> I know you're the kind of guy that can
>   make me reach my peak
> . . . .
> You make me cream and shout.[7]

Rock idol Prince has led the way toward explicitness, repeating the word "fuck" numerous times in "Erotic City."[8] Madonna has become the darling of hundreds of thousands of young girls, many not even in their teens, and the fantasy of many young boys. Her 1985 hit "Like a Virgin" has sold millions of copies. In the video for the song, Madonna writhes on a bed—a singing siren of seduction. In concert, she has been known to writhe on the stage and assume poses before her male guitar player suggestive of oral sex. Her message, in part, is that women can be as down-and-dirty lewd as male rock stars. *Rolling Stone* paints a vivid picture of what our teenagers and preteens see at a Madonna concert:

> Madonna was a sweaty pinup girl come to life. She wiggled her tummy and shook her ass. She smiled lasciviously and stuck out her tongue. She rolled around on the stage and got down on her knees in front of a guitarist. And when she raised her arms, her scanty see-through blouse also rose, revealing her

purple brassiere. . . . What Madonna is really about is sex, and there was plenty of that.[9]

Madonna has been singled out not so much because she dishes up more sex than other groups, but because her fans are so young. She belongs in a nightclub, but her audience is predominantly pre-teen. Like my antagonist at the NARAS forum, Wendy O. Williams, she has performed on stage in attire once reserved for burlesque theaters.

Members of Mötley Crüe, a band popular with young teens, thrive on explicitly describing sexual activities, in public. As part of their act, they have been known to shout into the microphone such statements as "Do you motherfuckers like to eat pussy? Do you know why our fuckin' hearts are broken tonight, Boston? Because we can't eat all that Boston pussy tonight."[10]

In most cases, the corporations sponsoring these performers are fully aware of what is going on. They back it because it makes money. Take, for example, Mötley Crüe's record company, Elektra/Asylum Records. A press release issued by the company for Mötley Crüe's *Shout at the Devil* commends the album to our children in this fashion: "Dripping with impure and adulterated lust and a take-no-shit-and-grab-some-tit attitude, *Shout at the Devil* is a call to arms for American youth." On the front page of the same release the record company brags about the band's lifestyle:

> Then there was the teenage girl who decided to hang out with the band for a few days in San Francisco. After playing tag team rude-and-lewd with her, she

insisted they each autograph her butt. They did and then she treated the entire road crew. She later showed up in Los Angeles, introduced herself to a record company executive and pulled her pants down. Their signatures were still there![11]

Even the most open-minded parent can still manage a blush—at least I hope!

If you think these performers care about what parents think of their excesses, you are mistaken. Some don't. Nikki Sixx, a member of Mötley Crüe, was interviewed by a teen magazine *(Creem)* about my concerns. (Italics in the following quotation differentiate the interviewer's comments from Sixx's.)

> *[Tipper Gore] read me this: "Here's what Motley Crue said from the stage . . . "Oh, we're so glad to be in Albuquerque. Our only regret is we can't eat all the pussy we see here tonight.' " Um . . . How do you respond?*
>
> (Laughs). You know what I say? I say fuck 'em. It's freedom of speech; First Amendment.
>
> *They're talking about their kids, though.*
>
> They must have had an awful sterile youth.

When the interviewer clarified my point, that there is a world of difference between the ability of an adult and a young teenager to cope with such statements, Sixx retorted, "Hey, if they wanna hide their heads in the sand and think that it's just beautiful and the yellow brick road's out there, the joke's on them."[12]

SEX AND VIOLENCE: COMBINED AND CONFUSED

The problem goes beyond lewdness. Parents must be even more concerned with the way some rock stars present sex itself to kids. Rock sensation David Lee Roth said of sadomasochism: "[S&M] is one of the last taboos that titillated the public. Now it's been made into a comic book, particularly with heavy metal."[13] Joe Stuessy points out that violence and the tools of violence are increasingly used as metaphors for sex. Consider the following examples of song lyrics:

Ted Nugent   Took her in the room with the mirrors on
              the walls,
            Showed her my brand new whip,
             . . . .
            Screamed as she started to slip.
            Give me a dose
            Of your violent love.
                               "Violent Love"[14]

Mötley Crüe   Slide down my knees, taste my sword.
               "Tonight (We Need a Lover)"[15]

            Touch my gun
            But don't pull my trigger
             . . . .
            Shine my pistol some more
             . . . .
            I got one more shot
            My gun's still warm.
                     "Ten Seconds to Love"[16]

Kiss   Cause when I go through her
            It's just like a
            Hot knife
            Through butter
                 "Fits Like a Glove"[17]

The Who   My love will cut you like a knife.
             "You Better You Bet"[18]

AC/DC   Let me cut your cake with my knife.
"Let Me Put My Love into You"

Shoot to thrill,
Way to kill,

. . . .
I got my gun at the ready,
Gonna fire at will.
"Shoot to Thrill"[19]

Judas Priest   Squealing in passion as the rod of steel
injects.
"Eat Me Alive"[20]

Great White   Gonna drive my love inside you
Gonna nail your ass to the floor.
"On Your Knees"[21]

Dokken   My barrel's ready,
My hand is steady

. . . .
I got my finger
It's on the trigger
Another night on the run.
"Bullets to Spare"[22]

According to Dr. Stuessy: "The metaphors describe the penis as a gun, a knife, a sword, a steel rod, a pipe; the vagina is a cake to be cut, or butter to be sliced; ejaculation is the act of shooting the gun; and semen consists of bullets."[23]

Stuessy continued that sure, some of the songs are open to interpretation. They can be about sex, murder, or both. For example, is AC/DC's "Shoot to Thrill" about sex or murder/suicide? Is Dokken's "Bullets to Spare" about sex or murder? With some songs, the metaphor is clear, for example, Mötley

Crüe's "Ten Seconds to Love," and "Tonight (We Need a Lover)"; for others, the total context encourages one interpretation over the other (e.g., "Bullets to Spare" *seems* to suggest sex rather than murder). "This ambiguity is very handy for the creator who, when challenged with an unfavorable interpretation, can assert that the real meaning simply escapes the simple mind of the perceiver! But this ambiguity, this confusion, is exactly the point. No question about it, the sex act is being equated with violence and pain."[24] They mix the two and make them synonymous. And these messages are marketed to our children without restraint.

For adults, confusion is usually not a problem. No song is likely to effect a modification in their sexual behavior. But what of the nine-, twelve-, or even sixteen-year-old who is forming his or her understanding of sexual morality and the very mechanics of sex itself?

Dr. Stuessy frames the question:

> But what if I were an impressionable fifteen-year-old boy today? My rock heroes have told me that sex on a date is expected and that it is a violent act. My penis is a knife, a gun, a rod of steel. Intercourse involves thrusting, plunging, screaming, and pain. My date is to be the object of my sexual cutting, slicing, and shooting. I must be very conscious of exerting my masculinity. I don't want my date, who, for all I know, is "experienced," to think I'm a wimp! I will nail her to the bed and make her scream in pain! Boy, this sex stuff is great!!

Can anything be worse than being a teenage girl, having to cope with teenage boys who are psychologically primed to cut, slice, and shoot with their "guns, knives, and swords"? Yes—being a teenage girl programmed to *accept* it.

Psychiatrists have told us for years that rape is not a sexual act, but an act of violence, at least in its motivation. In contrast to healthy sex, which is founded on love, respect, and responsibility, rape is an act of violence. But what do we now make of this confusion of violence and sex in today's music?

Stuessy acknowledges that sex is a delicate and touchy subject; first and foremost, it is private. Some advocate sex as pure pleasure, completely divorced from commitment or procreation, and in reality, both the sexual revolution and new birth control methods have helped to separate these two concepts. Parents make matters worse by avoiding the issue altogether. But to do their job well, parents must overcome any puritanical reluctance to communicate with their children about the full spectrum of sexual behavior. They need to be sure to emphasize that sex is part of love, not separate from it, and that love in turn requires one to be responsible for the consequences of sex. A child shouldn't be left in the dark just because his or her folks are embarrassed.

ADVERTISING MORE THAN JEANS

Just when you thought it was enough to turn down the radio, the blue jeans sex wars began on the pages of popular magazines. And they are nothing compared to the Calvin Klein–Perry Ellis perfume battle. Companies are betting big money on society's obsession with sex, as if all America were going through puberty.

In testing the public tolerance for quasi-pornographic ads, a handful of powerful interest groups are subtly altering the moral tenor of our culture.

In a way, advertisers are merely continuing a trend that began years ago, when fashion photographer Helmut Newton began shooting suggestive fashion layouts for *Vogue*. *Time* once labeled Newton the "King of Kink" for his provocative black-and-white photographs of nude women in bondage gear.[25] He began transposing a little of his avant-garde themes into the mass media market, making the general public a captive audience for his fetishes.

The sexy sell is nothing new. But increasingly, the target audiences are made up of eleven- and twelve-year-olds and teenagers of both sexes. A recent Swatch Watch ad, which I saw posted in a twelve-year-old girl's school locker, showed a young boy and a young girl, apparently unclothed but covered by a large sheet, doing their homework together in bed. It's small comfort to know that the advertiser is encouraging youth to do well in school, too.

Stan Gortikov of the RIAA was puzzled that the PMRC targeted recorded music, when so many advertisements were dripping with sexually explicit messages. He came to one meeting with a fistful of suggestive ads he had ripped from magazines, and threw them on the table among the explicit album covers. He had a good point. Today's youth are bombarded with sexual messages. If they watch television, listen to music, leaf through a magazine, or go to a movie, they will assuredly face the suggestion that sex at an early age is cool. The record seems to be stuck in one groove—sex.

Who can forget young Brooke Shields cooing: "Do you want to know what comes between me and my Calvin's? Nothing." That could have cost sales in the underwear department, but no, Klein blocked his own pass and developed even more suggestive ads to promote his line of designer underwear.

Klein launched a far more offensive first strike for his perfume, Obsession. The first printed advertisement for this product depicted a *menage-a-trois:* a nude woman flanked by two nude men. Another ad showed a man kissing a nude woman just below her breast, her nipple and bare breast in full view. In another we were treated to three nude women intertwined on the floor. All the ads were chic, artful, and arousing. But do they belong in the public domain? Are they appropriate for children as well as adults?

The late designer Perry Ellis followed suit in the ads for his new perfume for men. In one, a male model appears with a caption saying that he took the perfume bottle and then smiled his "best F--- you smile and walked out" (letters deleted in source). When several magazines refused to run the ad, its proponents countered that everyone on Madison Avenue talks that way.[26]

The jeans wars are back in full swing. Guess Fashions is taking on Jordache, with both peddling explicit sex with all the vigor and dedication of heavy metal rock stars. In 1986, Guess Fashions spent $10 million on advertising; they expect a $220 million return.[27]

Increasingly, these advertisements seem to incorporate private sexual fantasies. What else would provoke Guess' sexually ambiguous ads? Young girls are photographed in an embrace that suggests more than simple friendship. The new Guess ads "are moving toward what [the company's owner] calls 'more romance and friendship,' though many viewers may find the pictures of two young girls frolicking and embracing in a field have a strong lesbian undertone."[28] What can be next?

Competitive titillation seems to be driving these companies to greater and greater excess. They seem to give little thought to the effect of their advertisements on the moral fabric of society.

Offerings in the public domain should meet more scrupulous standards than what some may tolerate in the privacy of their homes. In America, morality has always been a matter of personal choice—not a commercial decision.

Where do we draw the line? Many people may not find nudity and sexual suggestiveness offensive. The question is how much sexual explicitness in advertising we, as a society, are willing to accept. Noting the trend toward using direct language in ads for such personal products as contraceptives, tampons, and douches, CBS vice-president Winifred Gorlin suggested, "We have to remember we're a guest in people's homes."[29] But that seems to be something the networks, publishers, and a number of advertising agencies and the companies they represent have obviously forgotten—or don't care about.

TEEN MAGAZINES

Can it get worse? Teen magazines, once the province of letters and articles about the stars' favorite colors, have changed drastically, too.

One teenybopper magazine presented its young readers with a Top Ten list rating the size of the genitals of certain male rock stars. The list, in the August 1986 *Metal Hotline*, was entitled "Who Has the Biggest Bulge [i.e., crotch] in Rock?"[30]

The May-June 1984 issue of *Rock Magazine* allowed John Crawford of the group Berlin to confess to his dream to sleep with Marie Osmond. "I know there is an animal pent up in that girl," he said, "which I could unleash anally."[31]

Even the most tolerant parents might question the propriety of publishing such anecdotes as the following, extracted from interviews of the band Mötley Crüe:

> We just flew in from Lubbock, Texas. . . .Man, there were some chicks there that were incredible. There was one who we got in the dressing room, and we were fucking her with this wine bottle—it was unbelievable. All her friends were standing around staring, but she was loving it. I mean she wasn't just taking the small end of the bottle. I only wish I had my Polaroid. I have a whole collection of groupie shots, and that one would have been the best.[32]

> The other day we had this one chick in the van and she was hanging over the seat naked. She was doing Nikki on one side, and we were shoving a beer bottle in her on the other side of the seat. It was great.[33]

> "It's a pretty hot album," Sixx agreed. . . . "We write really good songs. One of my favorites on the album is *Ten Seconds to Love*. If you listen very closely, you can hear a lot of squishy sounds during that song. That's because we were fucking some chicks while we were making the record. Now when they're playing

that song at home they can tell all their friends, "Hear that noise? That's me being fucked by Nikki Sixx."[34]

HIGH TECH SEX

The transmission of sounds, words, and images has been greatly facilitated by the vast technological changes that have occurred in the last twenty years. The technological developments of cable television, satellite communication, videotape recording, and the computer have significantly altered the production, distribution, and availability of sexually explicit materials.

In a recent issue of *Editorial Research Reports*, published by *Congressional Quarterly*, Harrison Donnelly explained the phenomenon of "high tech sex":

> While civil libertarians and their foes have been arguing over fine points of obscenity law, the technology for portraying explicit sex has been progressing rapidly, threatening to make much of their debate obsolete. New methods for delivering sexual materials directly into the home are making traditional controls on adult bookstores and movie theaters almost irrelevant. "High tech sex," as some have called it, is changing the pornography business as thoroughly as hard-core photographs and movies altered the age-old trade in "dirty books."[35]

A parent in Oak Ridge, Tennessee, recently wrote to tell me that her young daughter had received an unsolicited direct mail advertisement for pornographic films from "Kalbrus" in New York. "Here are our 12 most popular hard-core features," the ad proclaims, with a list of explicit pictures and paragraphs explaining the films. The company boasts that:

> BECAUSE we are the largest independent totally integrated facility in America and we just doubled our production capacity. WE CAN NOW. . .
> 1. Load empty cassette cases at a speed of 3600 T-120's/hour.
> 2. High-Speed duplication of these cassettes at a rate of 2700 T-120's/hour/rack.
> 3. A fully automated/computerized QTS (Quality Control System) with a cost savings of 4000 work hours/week.[36]

Sophisticated technology makes it possible to produce explicit materials more quickly and inexpensively.

Some telephone companies have become the latest technology-based businesses to profit from the commercialization of sex, by selling long distance service to firms charging for pornographic messages on toll numbers. Callers hear a graphic description of any cruel, kinky, or bestial act they choose.

IS THERE AN IMPACT?

Some argue that the pervasive messages about sexual activity aimed at young people through virtually all media have no impact. I am convinced that view is wrong. Just as we have seen the apparent link between the media cult of violence and an actual epidemic of violent behavior, so too there may be a link between pervasive sexual messages in the media and the way young people approach sex. They have bought the bill of goods.

Our teen pregnancy rate is the highest in the industrialized world. Every year, some thirty thousand girls fifteen and under get pregnant.[37] There are of course many reasons for the increase, but health care professionals believe that media messages are a factor.

Time magazine's December 9, 1985, cover story, "Children Having Children," reported that health care professionals and counselors working in the field believe the manner in which sex is portrayed in the media, including rock music, helps to form teenage attitudes toward sex.[38]

Media messages about sex have become more explicit and direct. Idolized stars flaunt it as never before and titillate their young fans with their own kind of sex education. And the kids are eating it up as fast as the adults.

Most young teens are eager to break free of the bonds their parents have imposed on them as children. They begin to question their parents' rules and values, and search for an identity separate from the family in which they have been secure. They are emotionally vulnerable, easily impressed, and their judgment and reasoning skills still have a long way to go before they will be equipped to make mature, critical, independent judgments. There is a tremendous difference in the cognitive skills of a thirteen-year-old and an eighteen-year-old. But the entertainment world seems to treat them all alike.

Where does that leave our children?

• Teenage sexual activity has doubled since 1971;

today, about 50 percent of unwed teenagers are sexually active. Furthermore, it is estimated that about 80 percent of the five million sexually active teenagers in the country do not use birth control techniques.[39]

● More than a million American teenagers—about one in ten—get pregnant each year.[40] Among the developed nations, only the United States has had an increase in teenage pregnancy, in recent years.[41]

● Some twenty-seven thousand new cases of sexually transmitted diseases occur every day in the United States, including genital herpes, gonorrhea, syphilis, venereal warts, and the deadly AIDS.[42]

● The abortion rate for teenagers in the United States stands as high or higher than the combined abortion and birth rates in countries such as Sweden, France, Canada, and England.[43]

TIME TO TAKE A STAND?

Human beings were created as "male and female," as sexual beings endowed with this gift of love and life, this marvelous cycle of pleasure and re-creation. The sexual instinct is the most powerful urge humans know and can bring the most intense ecstasy. Nothing is wrong with songs and other messages that celebrate love and sex, as long as those in the public domain remain within the reasonable restraints of our social customs and values.

No one should want a return to the sexual hypocrisy of the 1950s, which was unrealistic and often repressive. But the pendulum has swung too far in our time toward the hedonistic philosophy of "If it feels good, do it; if you want it, take it."

In any case, it is smart to question the wisdom of adolescent sex. For fourteen-, fifteen-, and sixteen-year-olds, sex may simply be too much, too soon.

PORN ROCK VERSUS HARD-CORE PORNOGRAPHY

Is there a connection between porn rock and hard-core pornography? Pornography has found or created a tremendous audience in this country, and has mushroomed into an estimated $8 billion per year business.[44] A flood of explicit material has inundated the American landscape and has spilled over into the world of children. So is porn completely benign, or does it have insidious effects on our children?

Pornography is difficult to legally define, much less control. Our attitudes toward it have become lax, and in the meantime, the market has continued to change. Now, a new brand of vicious, violent porn is peddled to more and more people for more and more money. Some who are complacent about soft-style porn are oblivious to the changes in the overall porn market. Neither will they recognize that there is a responsible, non-fanatical, growing concern over pornography, that can't be pinned on outdated images of high-collared prudish misfits attempting to Lysol the world. But the overwhelming media response to this legitimate concern seems to be "kill the messenger"—by ridiculing an outdated image. Some continue to lampoon and caricature the messengers as sexually repressed hysterics. They seem to have a stake in the triumph of their own prejudice, regardless of the new realities about the dark, violent, degenerate, and dangerous world of pornography, and its indirect impact on the tone of our society.

Hard-core porn now includes a lot of savagery and disrespect for life and human dignity. In a recent poll of *Women's Day* magazine readers, 90 percent of those who replied believe that pornography encourages violence against women.

It is important to note that there is a difference between wanting to restrain and control and wanting to suppress and censor. It's the difference between saying "Put the horse back in the barn" and "Burn the barn down." The loudest voices in the argument can be extremists on both ends of this issue. The sentiment of the vast majority of the people is in the middle. The anger and despair many in the middle of this spectrum feel about the tyranny of the Times Square mentality does not automatically translate into a demand for a bland social homogeneity. They simply protest the forced diet of sexual excess. Theirs is a protest against the ugly underbelly of society trying to force itself into the mainstream and thereby change our self-image. The deviant slowly becomes the norm if the apathy of the middle allows it to be so.

I hope that as the debate continues to heat up, the people in the middle who long for mechanisms for choice and restraint, but who are against censorship, will join in. If they don't, extremists on both sides of the issue will control the debate and perhaps its outcome. We will witness either the continuing

•

triumph of the cult of violence and pornography and all the social evils that would represent, or we will witness the average person, pushed by unrequited moral outrage, to support the more extreme movements toward censorship. How we deal with these dilemmas will affect our national character.

Therefore, people who are positioned in the middle of this spectrum should be active on these issues in their communities, because that is where mechanisms for choice will be formulated. Those who feel strongly about this problem have an obligation to assume leadership in this fight—they should come forward and seize the moment. For starters, they can publicly deplore excessive violence, wherever it is found. They can organize around the issue of the availability of explicit sex- and violence-oriented entertainment to young children and teenagers. They should act not because they are crusading antisex moralists, but because they care about the moral foundation of the society and about the context in which sexuality is publicly displayed, be it on the marquee or on the radio.

We have every right to decide what is and is not acceptable for the public environment in which we and our children must live. Mutual commitment to the common purpose motivates us to defend some truths and values against others. Moral commitment is more than just a mechanistic fulfillment of private ideals. In a democratic society, the will of the people is expressed through the political process, and through consensus community action. We have choices. We can take a stand.

5

Merchants of Death: Touting Teen Suicide

Think I'll buy a forty-four/Give 'em all a surprise./
Think I'm gonna kill myself,/ Cause a little suicide.

—"I Think I'm Going to Kill Myself," by Elton John[1]

Teenage suicide is now a national epidemic of tragic proportions, cutting a swath of grief through families in every socio-economic layer of our society. Teen suicide not only sacrifices young lives, but leaves family members and friends traumatized, grieving, and ridden with guilt.

The growing number of victims highlights this uniquely American problem. Our youth suicide rate is among the highest of all other industrialized nations. An estimated five thousand kids kill themselves each year—thirteen teens a day. Half a million others try but fail, according to Charlotte Ross, director of the Youth Suicide National Center in Washington, D.C.[2] A recent *Who's Who* survey of high school students found that 31 percent of high achievers had contemplated suicide, and 4 percent had tried it.[3]

Because suicide still carries a social stigma, families sometimes try to cover it up to avoid humiliation and embarrassment. In many states suicide also involves loss of insurance coverage, and in some cases raises the practical problem of determining whether the act was intentional or accidental. I have relied on the most recent, widely reported and accepted figures on the magnitude of the problem. The actual number is undoubtedly higher than reported.

Suicide is now the second major cause of death among adolescents, and in the fifteen-to-twenty-four-year-old age bracket has increased by 300 percent since 1950. Yet it remains the number one preventable cause of death. Some experts say that more suicide prevention work in high schools would not only help depressed students there, but would prevent later suicides in colleges. Others worry that increased attention to the topic would result in even more suicides.[4]

Despite the growing dimensions of this tragic problem, the concept of suicide is presented in songs like "Suicide's an Alternative/You'll Be Sorry" on the album *Suicidal Tendencies*. An alarming number of (primarily) heavy metal and mainstream stars sing about suicide as one way to deal with problems; some almost seem to promote it.

White males are most at risk for suicide. Young white males are also the primary audience for heavy metal music, with its predominant images of death and destruction. Many heavy metal bands specialize in "death metal," "trash metal," or "black metal" songs, which are morbidly preoccupied with themes of death, destruction, hopelessness, and suicide. What happens when a confused, depressed adolescent picks up the album *Suicidal Tendencies* and sees the cover photo of boys hanging upside down from a jungle gym, their arms tied behind their backs?[5] Or meditates on the cover of the band Accept's new album, *Russian Roulette*, which shows one young man, a gun in his hand, challenging another to join in the game?[6]

Would such a youth identify with such messages of doom as these lyrics from "Suicide's An Alternative/You'll Be Sorry":

> Sick of people—no one real;
> Sick of chicks—they're all bitches;
> Sick of you—you're too hip;
> Sick of life—it sucks. . . .
> Sick of life—it sucks;
> Sick and tired—and no one cares;
> Sick of myself—don't wanna live;
> Sick of living—gonna die.[7]

Perhaps we can find part of the reason for this despair in these lyrics from the same album:

> B-1 bombers in flight,
> Trident missiles in the air,
> MX missiles underground,
> Protect us till we're dead. . . .
> Mass starvation,
> Contaminated water,
> Destroyed cities,
> Mutilated bodies.
> I'll kill myself.
> I'd rather die.
> If you could see the future,
> You'd know why.[8]

"Suicidal Failure," also from this album, presents a hopeless outlook on life:

> Father forgive me
> For I know now what I do;
> I tried everything
> Now I'll leave it up to you.
> I don't want to live.
> I don't know why.
> I don't have no reasons,
> I just want to die.[9]

The group Metallica, which just produced their first gold album, *Master of Puppets* (half a million copies sold), hinted at suicide on an earlier album, *Ride the Lightning:*

> Life it seems, will fade away
> Drifting further every day
> Getting lost within myself
> Nothing matters, no one else
> I have lost the will to live
> Simply nothing more to give
> There is nothing more for me
> Need the end to set me free[10]

According to the National Education Association, "Many . . . teenage suicides are linked to depression fueled by fatalistic music and lyrics."[11] In late 1984, nineteen-year-old John McCollum shot himself in the head at his home in Indio, California. He had been listening to Ozzy Osbourne's albums before he killed himself, and was still wearing stereo headphones when his body was discovered. As the United Press International reported, "The lyrics in 'Suicide Solution' are part of what McCollum's parents claim spurred the teenager's suicide."[12]

Breaking laws, knocking doors
But there's no one at home
Made your bed, rest your head
But you lie there and moan
Where to hide, Suicide is the only way out
Don't you know what it's really about[13]

The father of the boy sued British rocker Osbourne and CBS Records for contributing to his son's death. Osbourne denied that his song promoted suicide and said that the bereaved parents had grossly misinterpreted his lyrics. He said "Suicide Solution" is really an antisuicide piece about a musician friend, Bon Scott, who died of acute alcohol poisoning in 1980. The word "solution," according to Osbourne's interpretation, means the liquid alcohol that caused Scott's death.[14] (Yet Osbourne has appeared in a fan magazine photograph holding a gun to his head.[15]) A trial judge dismissed the lawsuit on grounds that the lyrics are protected by the First Amendment. Is there no place for artistic and corporate responsibility and self-restraint? Is it responsible to promote teen suicide when we are in the midst of a national epidemic?

John McCollum's father had sued CBS to try to force the company to acknowledge responsibility for is own actions. "The record companies are more at fault than the artists," he says now. "They know what they are putting out. The producers who compile so many tracks of music, messages that are unbelievable—they know. The most important thing that I've learned is that there are people who are out there trying to make money, and they have no hesitation to sell your kids down the drain."[16]

PLANTING THE SEED OF SUICIDE

How suggestive—even directive—are Blue Oyster Cult's lyrics to "Don't Fear the Reaper" or the message of the song "Blessed Death" on their album of the same name? Might a few susceptible young people, attracted to such violent, negative music, act on its signals? Does a song like Black Sabbath's "Killing Yourself to Live" promote suicide?—"Pain, suffering, and misery,/It's not the way the world was meant./It's a pity that you don't understand,/Killing yourself to live."[17]

In April 1986, I received a letter from Sandy Hanson of Colorado. Her son had just committed suicide and she had just discovered his music collection. She sent the *Suicidal Tendencies* album and had this to say: "It's not that I think music is the only cause. There are so many other factors such as: broken homes, peer pressure, problems with parents, the world political situation, grades. . . . I do feel if youth are particularly troubled, the music may have tremendous influence on them. They may not think of suicide otherwise."

The violent and jarring songs of the Australian heavy metal band AC/DC may be interpreted by young people as suicide lyrics. The parents of sixteen-year-old Steve Boucher, who put a gun to his forehead and blew out his brains, point to their son's obsession with negative music like the AC/DC song "Shoot to Thrill." He died under that band's poster-calendar, which hung on the wall in his room.[18]

Another sixteen-year-old, Dennis Bartts, hung himself from the goalposts of the football field at the

Center Point, Texas, high school. He had told his best friend that he "planned to meet Satan." He killed himself while listening to AC/DC's *Highway to Hell*, which he had carried with him on his cassette tape recorder.[19]

Rock music also provided the backdrop when eighteen-year-old Philip Morton hanged himself from a closet door in Delafield, Wisconsin, in February 1986. A human skull and a burning candle stood near the body of the St. John's Military Academy cadet. A tape of Pink Floyd's album *The Wall*, which includes the songs "Is There Anybody Out There?", "Goodbye Cruel World," and "Waiting for the Worms," had been playing continuously.

The Delafield chief deputy medical examiner, Paul Hibbard, noted that the album's lyrics may have set the mood for the suicide. "My personal feeling is that this type of music is going to add to the depression," he told the *Milwaukee Journal*. "If they're depressed, this music is going to send them deeper. And if [Philip Morton] wanted to change his mind sometime during this, the music wouldn't help."[20]

Another set of parents, Jean and Elmer Fisk of San Pablo, California, believe the song "Suicide Solution" had something to do with their son's suicide in October 1985. Jean Fisk sent this heart-rending letter to the PMRC office:

> My son died in April of 1983; he was a teen suicide. He was 6 weeks away from high school graduation in the top 5% of his class. He took 4 years of math, science, French, English, and other requirements to get into a top-notch college. He was accepted at the college of his choice. His math teacher told us he had

the finest mathematical brain the teacher had worked with in 10 years. He was the only student in his high school of over 2,000 recommended by his chemistry teacher to participate in a U. C. Berkeley Chemistry summer work-and-learn program. He was also the only photographer in the area to have an award-winning photo (that he took and developed) selected by the Photographers' Society of America Young Photographer's Showcase traveling display throughout the USA for one year. He had had perfect attendance in school every year since 7th grade. The autopsy showed no trace of any alcohol or drugs of any kind. He did not use drugs or smoke anything.

When my husband and I were going through his papers after he died, we found the words to a rock song, "Suicide Solution." We asked his girl friend about the words and she told us it was his favorite song. I feel that these words opened up a tragic alternative to him that he would not have otherwise considered. . . .

My son was not perfect. He had to be told several times to take out the garbage etc., but he did have a bright future ahead of him. If the control of this type of rock music prevents even one loss, one family from this devastating grief, then is it not worth the effort? I hope other parents wake up and listen to the words before it is too late. I only wish I had.

Yet another report of a suicide came to the nation's attention in a story first carried by the *Gazette Journal* of Sparks, Nevada:

The mother of an 18-year-old Sparks man who shot himself to death in a double suicide pact sued the heavy metal rock group Judas Priest on Thursday, saying their music led her boy to kill himself. . . .
The suit said Belknap's suicide "was precipitated by

the lyrical instructions of the music he was listening to just before his death and at the time of his death that created an uncontrollable impulse to commit physical harm to oneself or suicide."[21]

For six hours straight, Raymond Belknap and James Vance had been smoking pot in Belknap's bedroom and listening to Judas Priest's album *Stained Class*, containing the song "Heroes End." The two boys left through a window when Belknap's mother returned, taking a shotgun with them. At a neighborhood playground the two shot themselves. One died; the other survived a severe wound to the face. The boy who lived has said that the music lulled them into thinking that "the answer to life is death."[22]

CLUSTER SUICIDES: A DISTURBING TREND

Teen suicides often occur in clusters—human dominoes falling in quick succession. One young person in a community will commit suicide and within a few days, another youth will take his or her life, then another, and another. In some instances, these kids don't even know each other and share no connections aside from living in the same town, attending the same school, and seeing the same reports of one another's deaths. Analysts are taking a closer look at the role of media influences in these serial suicides.

In February 1986, Bryan High School in Omaha, Nebraska, suffered three suicides in a period of five days. Four other students had attempted suicide during the preceding three weeks. The principal told

Time magazine, "We have a 'life is cheap' philosophy fed to the young." He pointed to pro-suicide rock lyrics as a particular example of this.[23]

If suicide *is* contagious, a rock band's mesmerizing suicidal imagery might just be enough to topple some of its youthful listeners. In the words of Jean Fisk, it opens up "a tragic alternative" they might not otherwise have been considering.

A few artists are sensitive to the teen suicide epidemic and have addressed it responsibly and carefully in song. Debby Boone's "Choose Life" and Billy Joel's moving single and video "You're Only Human" deliver a strong antisuicide message. These positive efforts are to be commended.

CATALYST FOR SUICIDE

We cannot help but notice the same kind of music figuring in case after case of teenage suicide. Steve Boucher was attracted to AC/DC's "Shoot to Thrill"; John McCollum was tuned into Ozzy Osbourne's "Suicide Solution"; Philip Morton was playing Pink Floyd's *The Wall*. True, millions of kids listen to these songs and don't kill themselves, but that doesn't change the fact that there have been too many suicides by teens who were fascinated by this suicide-obsessed music.

Many other parents of teens who attempted suicide have contacted the PMRC after discovering the degree to which their children have been immersed in negative music. Most teens do not listen repeatedly to heavy metal music, do not take it seriously, and reject the horribly negative groups. But some kids are tuned in to "death metal" and "black

Examples of explicit violence from the popular teen slasher *Friday the 13th* movies—soon to be made into a television series.

Severed torso of young lover

Teen victim knifed from back

Stills from *Friday the 13th: Part 3*. A Jason, Inc.—Frank Mancuso, Jr., Production; a Steve Miner Film. Copyright © 1982 Jason Productions, Inc. Copyright © 1983 Paramount Pictures Corp.

Wendy O. Williams argues, "Rock and roll has always been aggressive, raw and sexual in its attitude."

Photo by Lynn Goldsmith. *Hit Parader*, April 1983.

Hit Parader's Heavy Metal Hot Shots, September 1985.

"The boys get their kicks on the road" is how *Hit Parader* describes this Judas Priest promotional shot.

Examples of explicit sexual violence from the movie *I Spit on Your Grave,* available from video stores with only an R rating.

One of several gang rape scenes

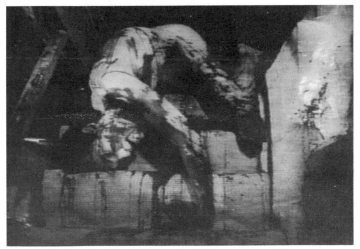

Scene of victim who bled to death from castration

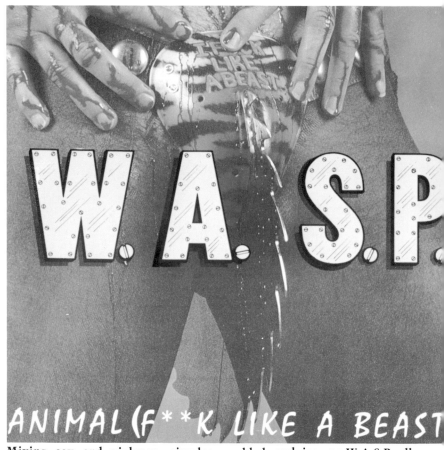

Mixing sex and violence—circular saw blade codpiece on W.A.S.P. album, *Animal (F**k Like a Beast)*.

Photo by David McGough/DMI. *Hit Parader*, August 1983.

In the face of a national epidemic of teen suicide, Ozzy Osbourne claims his song "Suicide Solution" does not promote suicide.

Detail of fan's shirt on the cover of the *Suicidal Tendencies* album.

Promotion photo of members of the band Metallica in a teen magazine.

Rock group Mötley Crüe pretending to snort cocaine in a teen fan magazine.

Concert stars in action . . .

Creem Rock-Shots, October 1985.

Photo by Annamaria DiSanto. Creem Rock-Shots Presents Van Halen & David Lee Roth: The Noise & the Fury,

Rock idol Madonna performs on stage for a teen and preteen audience.

Sammy Hagar of the band Van Halen on stage with his Jack Daniel's: "I trust that none in this audience consider me a so-called 'role model'!"

metal." Many of those who do listen to a great deal of negative music are troubled, and their interest in the music should be a warning sign to adults.

Several respected researchers recently found that even the *publicity* about teenage suicides causes some teens to consider it. If simple news coverage pushes some kids over the edge, what should an intelligent person think about lyrics that glorify and even promote a truly dead end?

MEDIA THAT CAN KILL

Two new studies published in the *New England Journal of Medicine* in September 1986 specifically link television coverage of suicide in movies or news reports with the incidence of teenage suicide.

Dr. David P. Phillips and Lundie L. Carstensen, researchers at the University of California at San Diego, released a study which found that the national rate of suicide among teenagers rises significantly just after television news or feature stories about suicide.[24]

Columbia University announced another study, authored by Dr. Madelyn S. Gould and David Shaffer, which also systematically documented evidence that suicides and suicide attempts increased dramatically in a two-week period immediately following the showing on television of four fictional movies about suicide. Dr. Gould said that the study did not determine if the victims had actually seen the movies, except in the case of one seventeen-year-old New York boy who watched and then copied the manner of suicide shown in the movie.[25]

"One of the theories," Dr. Phillips told the *Atlanta*

113

Constitution, "is that the publicized story gives others 'permission' to do the same thing. 'Gee [thinks the teen], I thought I was the only person who was feeling this bad. I don't feel like such an oddball. I'm not the only one who has ever thought of [suicide].' "[26] Other reports of suicides seem to lend credence to his theory. One fifteen-year-old suicide victim was found dead, with a newspaper report of another child suicide taped to the headboard of her bed, where her body was found.[27]

PREVENTION BEGINS AT HOME

Adults need to understand the dimensions of the teenage suicide crisis and be ready to help. Many factors contribute to suicide, and all should be seriously and promptly addressed, especially those pertaining to the home environment and the quality of the relationship between parent and child. Dr. Mark Rosenberg, chief of the violence epidemiology branch of the Centers for Disease Control, puts the task succinctly: "We have to rethink youth suicide. . . . We need to look at the causes, people at risk, how you identify it and strategies for prevention."[28]

The religious and educational communities need to get the message to our young that they have a future to look forward to, that there are alternatives to suicide, that life is too sacred to throw away. Parents, churches, synagogues, and schools can start by pointing out the dangers of negative media messages and by encouraging young people to adopt discriminating listening and viewing habits. Most important, parents should *spend time* with their children.

114

Kids themselves should be encouraged to talk to a responsible adult—a parent, pastor, rabbi, or teacher—if one of their friends is troubled and thinking of suicide. And *everyone* should learn the warning signs of suicide.

Adolescence is the most difficult period of human development. While crises occur at each stage of life, teenagers are the least equipped to deal with this rapid growth period on their own. It is at this time that they most need love, guidance, and supervision. The father of the late John McCollum agrees that adult involvement in children's lives is a must. As he told me: "If we can just save one life, it will be worthwhile. It is hard for me to believe that what has happened to my son actually did happen to him. It is important for parents to wake up."[29]

JUST IN CASE

Here is a checklist, recommended by mental health professionals, for parents to use in determining whether their children might be considering suicide, or might be especially vulnerable to any suicidal suggestions.

1. Watch for any radical personality change; take signs of depression seriously. Children should not be depressed for unusual lengths of time. Obviously, they will experience mood swings; it's normal for teens to be depressed at times. You must judge what is normal and what is not, for your child, based on your familiarity with his or her personality.

2. Watch for an abandonment of favorite activities or people.
3. Watch for listlessness and expressions of feelings of worthlessness, such as "I'm no good; I'm a failure."
4. Take note of a marked withdrawal from the family or close associates.
5. Note changes in sleeping or eating habits, in the direction of either too much or too little.
6. Check for falling grades and classes being cut.
7. Note any violent or extremely rebellious behavior.
8. Watch for drug or alcohol use. This is very important, because a teen seriously caught up in drug or alcohol abuse is already living in an altered state of reality which will impair his or her thinking skills.
9. Be aware that certain physical symptoms are often related to emotional stress, such as stomachaches and recurrent headaches.
10. Listen for expressions of desire for death. A teenager who is really planning to take his life may also: (1) hint about it; (2) give away favorite possessions; (3) exhibit inappropriate cheerfulness in the midst of depression.
11. Be alert to depression over the death of a friend or relative.
12. Find out what your children are reading, listening to on albums, and watching at the movies or on television.

6

Playing with Fire: Heavy Metal Satanism

Let's say a really great group emerged . . . and they came out with a really great album and turned a lot of people on to Satanism. There's got to be a point where you're gonna say, "Look, guys, we're all for artistic freedom, but maybe we just don't want de debbil trampling across America."

—Paul McCartney[1]

Everyone loves a magic show. Bored with the straightforward adult world, children in particular are mesmerized by the mystical and the unexplained. This childhood fascination with the occult has led to one of the most sickening marketing gimmicks in history. Just as some in the music industry emphasize sex or violence in their songs, others, especially certain heavy metal groups, sell Satan to kids. The demonic, it turns out, is a lucrative—and dangerous—trademark. By using satanic symbols on the concert stage and album covers, such as those employed by Ozzy Osbourne, Ronnie James Dio, and groups like Venom, Slayer, Black Sabbath, Mötley Crüe, Celtic Frost, Mercyful Fate, W.A.S.P., and Iron Maiden, certain heavy metal bands lure teenagers into what one expert has called "the cult of the eighties."[2] Many kids experiment with the deadly satanic game, and some get hooked.

The devil has turned up in rock music before, in more innocuous forms. In the late sixties, the Rolling

Stones cut an album entitled *Their Satanic Majesties Request,* and later a song called "Sympathy for the Devil." As Professor Joseph Stuessy points out, such references are merely spiritual or literary allusions, no more serious than Liszt's "Mephisto Waltz." Like astrology or transcendental meditation, he says, the satanism in sixties songs represented a "fleeting curiosity about alternate philosophies and religions."[3]

But like a cancer, satanism has come a long way since then, as heavy metal groups capitalized on a growing fascination with the occult. From *The Exorcist* to the Dungeons and Dragons fantasy role-playing game, Americans chased one occult fad after another. The popular Dungeons and Dragons game has sold eight million sets. The game is based on occultic plots, images, and characters which players "become" as they play the game. According to Mrs. Pat Pulling, founder of the organization Bothered About Dungeons and Dragons, the game has been linked to nearly fifty teenage suicides and homicides. Pulling's own son killed himself in 1982 after becoming deeply involved in the game through his school's gifted students program. A fellow-player threatened him with a "death curse," and he killed himself in response.

The advent of satanic rock has introduced the accoutrements of satanism to a generation of kids. It is being pushed aggressively because the companies have found the commercialization of satanism to be profitable. Consider this advertisement from RCA records for the heavy metal band Grim Reaper.

Grim Reaper is Going to Send You Straight to HELL. Grim Reaper is coming to mow you down with heavy metal so intense it'll scare the hell out of you. Their album "SEE YOU IN HELL" has already taken possession of the top of the English charts, and now America is next to feel the heat. . . . [It's] THE ALBUM YOU'LL SELL YOUR SOUL FOR.[4]

If it were nothing more than commercial fantasy, as transparent and foolish as professional wrestling, heavy metal satanism would be easy to overlook. The success of movies like *The Exorcist, The Omen,* and *Poltergeist* proves how much people like to be scared to death. But many would argue that although people define it in many different ways, there really is a struggle between good and evil, and that as a result, it is not harmless and trivial to glamorize evil. Not everyone can see through the show-biz satanism purveyed by more and more bands. Many young fans are tempted to experiment with the satanic practices the bands describe, and some troubled or bored teens go much farther. Whether or not the bands are themselves serious about satanism, the image they project can have a serious impact on some of their young fans. As reporter Tom Jarriel on ABC's "20/20" said, "The Satanic message is clear, both in the album covers and in the lyrics, which are reaching impressionable young minds."[5]

Some band members defend satanism as a harmless game. King Diamond, lead singer of the now defunct Mercyful Fate, told a radio interviewer, "Satan simply deals in magic, which is merely an entertaining, fun thing."[6] Small comfort—but several bands go to great lengths to prove that their occult interest is for real by writing about explicit satanic practices in their lyrics. Professor Stuessy considers some of these explicit songs almost evangelical. When the band Venom sings "Sacrifice," Stuessy says, "the effect on some impressionable teens is that of a play-by-play prescription for a satanic ritual":

> Sacrifice,
> Oh so nice. . .
> Sacrifice to Lucifer, my master.
> Bring the chalice,
> Raise the knife,
> Welcome to my sacrifice;
> Plunge the dagger in her breast,
> I insist.
> S-a-c-r-i-f-i-c-e. . .
> Demons rejoice,
> Sacrifice, sacrifice,
> Name your price.[7]

The jacket copy for the album *Welcome to Hell*, also by Venom, includes the following poem:

> We're possessed by all that is evil
> The death of you, God, we demand
> We spit at the virgin you worship
> And sit at Lord Satan's left hand.[8]

Other groups convey much the same message. Consider Slayer's *Reign in Blood*. A reviewer for *SPIN* magazine described the album as "an Evelyn Wood speed-listening course on satanism, death, and hell."[9] The album was rife with sadistic and Nazi-inspired imagery; Columbia Records pulled out of a deal to release it.[10] The song "Necrophiliac," found on an earlier Slayer album, reveals lyrics dedicated to satanism:

120

I feel the urge,
The growing need,
To fuck this sinful corpse;
My task's complete,
The bitch's soul
Lies raped in demonic lust.[11]

Many teens are drawn to this bizarre occult subculture. As fantasies go, satanism has everything—strange symbols, mysterious rituals, a secret code. At the same time, it is perhaps the ultimate form of rebellion. It rejects Judeo-Christian religion, turns good and evil upside down, and rebels against life itself. The kid who goes along with Venom's "We spit at the virgin you worship" can be reasonably sure that his or her folks would not approve.

But the "road to hell" is paved with perils. As in any cult, those who dabble in the satanic sometimes find it difficult to turn back. These teens are literally playing with fire.

SATANIC VIOLENCE ATTRACTS POLICE ATTENTION

Cleo Wilson is a detective with the Denver, Colorado, Police Department and a specialist in occult crime. She observed a disturbing increase in occult activity over the past six years. In February 1986 she investigated a ritualistic murder in which the victim had drunk his own blood.[12] A partner of hers, cult expert Detective Bill Wickersham, estimates that occult incidents, primarily animal slaughter and mutilation, have increased by 50 percent over the past five years. The police can do little to stop these practices on their own, Wilson says: "We don't want any hysteria. We don't want to label anything a witch hunt, because this *is* a religion. We cannot attack a belief system, so it ties our hands, really." While many satanic rituals, such as those involving cruelty to animals, are generally against the law, satanism itself is protected by the First Amendment right to freedom of religion.

"We are seeing more and more teens get into this," says Wilson. "These children aren't stupid. In fact, many are very bright. They're *bored*." She believes that occult fantasies give kids an opportunity to control their environment. "Kids feel very powerless," she says. "They deal in doom and death a lot—it's offered to them. It's glorified in this music, and it is also a reality they grew up with in the nuclear age."

Detective Wickersham agrees that occultism offers a violent escape from a violent world. "One of the philosophies to come out of the [threatened] nuclear holocaust is, 'Live for today because there is no tomorrow,' " he says. "The message in some of this music is that the world is going to end, so take what you can now and hurt who you want to."[13]

Most teens who try it end up only hurting themselves. Aside from bent value systems, perhaps the greatest danger of the occult boom is its association with teen suicide. Wickersham blames parents for letting kids get that far. "There are kids who commit suicide who are heavily involved in the occult and parents don't even know it," he says. "Kids' bodies are found, and you look around their room and see duct tape on the walls shaped like the inverted crosses that represent the antichrist. Parents have no idea what these things mean."

More often than not, when teens gather to indulge in the occult, heavy metal is there. According to Dann Cuellar, a television reporter in San Antonio who has investigated several recent satanic crimes, "The link we've found between kids and satanism is the music." Cuellar blames bands for glamorizing the occult. "Whether it is their intention or not to actually get people involved with it, that is exactly what's happening."[14] Cult expert Sandi Gallant of the San Francisco Police Department agrees. "No matter what heavy metal band leaders say," she says, "they are projecting an image to the kids that they are satanists. Children want to emulate their stars."

Cuellar believes that most teens don't always know what satanic music is about. "To them it's just a game, a fad," he says. Most kids don't take it beyond that." But a few, perhaps 5 percent by Cuellar's estimate, take enough interest to look into it further. Many buy or steal from the public library or bookstore a copy of *The Satanic Bible* by Anton La Vey.

The satanism that teens toy with is often linked to religious desecration, satanic graffiti, and animal theft and mutilation. In October 1985 the Society of Animal Welfare Administrators met in Colorado to discuss their concern about the growing number of animal mutilations. Dann Cuellar described a mutilated horse found in the middle of a red pentagram spray-painted on the street of a Texas city. A police detective in Denver described the discovery of a calf that had been bled and then abandoned in a trash dumpster, still alive.[15] In Greeneville, Tennessee, the sheriff's office investigated reports of high school students' and several adults' involvement in a satanic worship service that included animal sacrifice and bathing in blood. According to Bill Solomon, Sheriff's Deputy Investigator in Greeneville, Tennessee, the teens got the idea from satanic music and from witchcraft books they stole from the public library. "The biggest majority are fooling around with it," he says, "but they don't know what they are getting into. And with live sacrifices, it gets serious."[16] Professor Stuessy found that "in virtually every case, the names of the rock groups or their songs are associated with such atrocities." While music is not the only influence, he says, it is a contributing factor.

BLOOM COUNTY   **by Berke Breathed**

PARENTS, TAKE NOTE

Satanism has been around for thousands of years and it is unlikely to disappear any time soon. The best way to counter this or any other cult is to give children something better to believe in. "Kids are out there raising themselves," says Sandi Gallant. "We must give them something to use their energy and give their lives meaning."

Parents must take their children's interests seriously. The radical evolution of heavy metal shows how far kids must go to shock parents who try to ignore them. One mother in San Antonio, Texas, noticed her eldest son "doing rather bizarre things" but she tried to respect "his private space." When an animal sacrifice blood-drinking ritual frightened him back to reality, she learned just how troubled the teen had been.

Perhaps the simplest way to dispose of heavy metal demons is to explain what they represent. Bill Wickersham heard his eight-year-old daughter singing Ozzy Osbourne lyrics that she had picked up from other kids at school. "I took her to the record store and showed her his album covers," he recalls. "I said to her, 'This is Ozzy Osbourne. This is what he is about. Do you want that?' She thought he was really sick."

The Medium Is the Mixer: Alcohol and Drugs in Entertainment

After you're done relaxing you can drink a lot. Drink and bone massive amounts of women. In that order, because some girls look a little better when you're high.

—Mick Mars of the band Mötley Crüe[1]

BAD MODELS MAKE FOR BAD HABITS

Today, with alcohol and drug abuse at epidemic proportions in our country, hard rock bands continue to sing about, and in their concerts even demonstrate, the glories of drinking and getting high on drugs. An Associated Press poll revealed that 77 percent of the people surveyed believed that rock lyrics promote drug use.[2] Whatever the actual effect of these messages, the lyrics of many songs certainly seem to encourage the use—and abuse—of alcohol and other drugs. Furthermore, many musicians live the lives they sing about, presenting destructive public models for the young people who adore their music and idolize them. The drug-use messages that the Woodstock generation of rock bands began to convey fifteen years ago continue today, with more explicit lyrics than ever, and with alcohol and drugs being used more frequently as props for certain bands' raucous concerts. As AC/DC urges its listeners:

Whiskey, gin, and brandy
With a glass are pretty handy;
Tryin' to walk a straight line
On some . . . cheap wine. . . .
Come on, have a good time
And get blinded out of your mind,
So don't worry about tomorrow,
Take it today.
Forget about the tip,
We'll get hell to pay.
Have a drink on me.[3]

Young people listen to AC/DC's song in a country where alcohol remains the drug of choice; where one in sixteen high school seniors drinks alcohol daily, half of them to excess; where most of those started using alcohol between the ages of eleven and fourteen; where by ages fourteen to seventeen some three million young persons have experienced problems with alcohol.[4]

When our children get out the Black Sabbath album *Born Again*, they can listen to "Trashed," about drinking bottles of whiskey and tequila while driving down the road at 105 miles an hour. Does Black Sabbath care that the single leading cause of death among fifteen- to twenty-four-year-olds is drunk driving, that 50 percent of all highway deaths are alcohol related?[5] Is the band aware that the 1983 FBI report on crime showed that over a third of all arrests for drunk driving involved persons under twenty-five?[6]

Listening to the album *High 'n' Dry*, our youngsters hear the band Def Leppard sing:

A Saturday,
I feel alright,
I've been drinking all day. . . .
I got my whiskey, got my wine. . . .
Saturday night. . .
I'm high.[7]

Or if they go to see Mötley Crüe in concert, they might see band members brandish bottles of Jack Daniel's whiskey. Rock singer David Lee Roth has bragged in a fan magazine, "The Jack Daniels I drink on stage is real."[8]

How many children have followed this idolized role model and become one of the three out of ten youth in grades seven through twelve defined as problem drinkers? How many become binge drinkers—getting drunk on five or more drinks at least once every two weeks? How many of them will become another of the growing number of "early starters," the Alcoholics Anonymous designation for preteen and teenage alcoholics? How many will emulate Journey's "Lay It Down" lyrics: "Whiskey, wine and women,/They get me through the night. . . ./What I'm really needin',/Ah, double shot tonight"?[9] How many will grow up to join the ranks of the millions of adult alcoholics?

What do our children think when they hear Nikki Sixx of Mötley Crüe say: "My bottle of Jack Daniels is my best friend in the world. It's always there to give me support, even when my friends aren't. I can drink two or three bottles a day."[10] The record liner on Mötley Crüe's *Shout at the Devil* album carries the notation "This album was recorded on Foster's Lager, Budweiser, Bombay Gin, lots of Jack Daniels, Kalua and Brandy."[11] Mötley Crüe's lead singer Vince Neil was in a tragic automobile accident in 1984 which killed Nicholas "Razzle" Dingley, the drummer of the band Hanoi Rocks, and injured two other people. After Neil was convicted of vehicular manslaughter, Sixx's comments about drinking changed somewhat. Speaking for the band, he told an interviewer for *Creem* magazine: "We don't represent sobriety, we just don't want to see somebody have so much fun they kill themselves. . . . All we're saying is: get fucked up, do anything you wanna do with your life—that's fine, y'know . . . just don't get behind a wheel when you do it."[12] His anti-drunk driving message seems half-hearted, to say the least.

Kerrang!, a rock magazine imported from Britain and sold in the U.S., carried a photograph of Mötley Crüe pretending to snort cocaine, apparently celebrating the use of that dangerous drug?[13] That endorsement will hardly help our children through what *Newsweek* called "an authentic national crisis"—the war on drugs.[14]

"Children live in a world barraged by information and cues about drugs," Dr. Miller Newton told the *New York Times* in 1984. Author of the book *Not My Kids*, a parents' guide to children and drugs, Dr. Newton indicated that much of today's rock music includes "a constant stream of messages about getting high, feeling good, going on 'trips' and using drugs of all kinds with all methods."[15]

Drug use by some rock stars is no secret in the music world. In an overstatement, Kevin Dubrow, of the band Quiet Riot, said, "As far as the drug business, I mean, everybody in rock 'n' roll does drugs."[16] Tony Sanchez graphically described drug use on the rock scene in his book *Up and Down with the Rolling Stones:*

> Drugs were everywhere on this tour—jars of cocaine, uppers and downers. Jagger snorted quantities of coke before every show; he felt he couldn't get up there to dance and scream without the high of the drug tearing through his body. Keith fixed so much heroin that on stage he was an eerie, shambling wreck—everybody's idea of a freaked-out, druggie rock superstar—and the kids loved him for it.[17]

After songwriter/studio musician Michael Rudetsky died in August 1986 of respiratory failure caused by drugs (at the home of rock star Boy George, who was himself undergoing treatment at that time for heroin addiction), his friend Mark Berry wrote in *Billboard* magazine:

> I blame the institutionalization of drugs within our industry. . . . I blame people behind the scenes who, at best, turn their heads at recording sessions, rehearsals, and in backstage dressing rooms, and, at worst, supply tired, pressured performers with whatever they need to "get them through the night."[18]

Berry also blamed a misguided public that cheered when Janis Joplin (who died of drug and alcohol abuse in 1970) drank from a bottle as she performed. He called for "a new peer pressure . . . within our industry" and a new fashion of being drug-free—and alive.[19]

A WORD OF THANKS

Not all the messages coming from rock bands have touted alcohol and drug use. Some rock stars and bands have consistently sought to uplift while entertaining. Moreover, others have tried to reform. Actual disaster apparently changed the attitude of Johnny Rotten, former member of the now-defunct Sex Pistols, one of the leading bands of the early punk rock movement. After the widely publicized violent and drug-related death of Sid Vicious, Rotten (who now goes by his given name of John Lydon) strongly denounced rock bands that glorify the drug culture. Too many heavy metal bands, he said, promote "good weed, booze and lots of drugs," and he noted that listeners try to imitate what they hear and see.[20]

Singer Melba Moore, in the September 20, 1986, issue of *Billboard*, denounced the glorification of drugs by entertainers. "We can help set a moral example," she writes. "Performing is like being invited into someone's home. You have a personal effect on your audience, and they on you. So it is our responsibility to make sure our messages remain clear and positive."[21]

More recently, in the wake of the upsurge of national sentiment against drug abuse, record executive Danny Goldberg organized an effort called Rock Against Drugs (RAD), to present antidrug messages on MTV from rock stars such as Gene Simmons of Kiss and Vince Neil of Mötley Crüe.[22]

I applaud those rock artists and bands who seek to discourage destructive behavior and delinquent activities such as drug use. I hope their messages will make an impression on listeners, and have a special influence on those rock bands that now incorporate into their music one of the subculture's big themes: "Enjoy drugs."

PROMOTING CHEMICAL ABUSE

In my own travels and in my communications with people all across the country, I have found a deep concern about this problem and about the pro-alcohol and other pro-drug messages of too much rock music. Country music also contains many favorable references to alcohol, but by and large, young kids are not the mainstay of that particular genre's audience. President Reagan, in announcing plans for a new national strategy against illegal drugs, pointed directly to the influence of rock music on drug use. When *Newsweek* interviewed President Reagan on his views about the country's drug problem and asked why drugs are currently such a problem, the president replied: "For one thing . . . the music world . . . made it sound as if it's right there and the thing to do. . . . Musicians that young people like . . . make no secret of the fact that they are users."[23]

Initiatives against drugs and drug messages in music are not new. The Federal Communications Commission back in 1970 issued a directive to radio stations aimed at curbing lyrics that highlighted the use of drugs. The directive simply reiterated what all of us should already know—that the airwaves belong to the public and that stations are responsible for their programming, including songs promoting drug use. The directive clearly frightened the stations by suggesting that airing songs about drug use could raise "serious questions as to whether continued operation of the station is in the public interest." In an unfortunate overreaction, one station banned all of Bob Dylan's records, saying it could not possibly interpret his lyrics.[24]

For a time, this directive heightened public awareness of the drug culture's influence on rock music, and vice versa; then the campaign sputtered out and was all but forgotten. No new activity related to that directive has appeared recently.

Since 1970, efforts to curb drug use and to help those entangled in drug addiction fell to government and private agencies specifically dealing with drug trafficking, and to religious organizations, which continued to denounce the evils that alcohol and drugs bring to persons and to society. During this period, many rock bands projected glamorized messages urging their youthful listeners to join them in drinking bouts or to get high on illegal drugs.

In addition, rock concerts provide the alcohol industry with an ideal way to reach potential young customers. For example, some alcoholic beverage companies underwrite the cost of certain concert tours. Such financial underwriting of concerts is not a new arrangement, but now it gives alcohol advertisers an opportunity to reach teenagers and even preteens. These youngsters watch stars strut about the stage while chugging alcohol, glamorizing it at a time when alcohol use and abuse among young people is rising.

Some rock musicians blatantly publicize particular brands of whiskey. A member of the band Van Halen plays a guitar shaped like a Jack Daniel's bottle, which has been displayed to thousands of young people in concert acts and fan magazine pictures. Such an endorsement of alcohol use and abuse by revered rock stars carries a powerful wallop to impressionable minds.

Dr. Carl Taylor, an assistant professor of criminal justice at Michigan State University and also president of Centrax Services, Inc., a Detroit security company that has worked over five hundred traveling rock and roll shows, agrees that the bands' promotion of alcohol encourages an alcohol-based lifestyle.

> Alcohol is accepted among the adult population. Sure the rock stars promote it; it's free advertising. If a star pulls out a bottle of Jack Daniel's and drinks it on stage, the police won't arrest him because cops accept alcohol. It's different if that star gets up on stage and lights up a joint, but the kids in the audience are already doing that. People don't seem to realize that these stars are promoting a lifestyle. They're dictating a lifestyle to the kids, who say, "If this guy drinks Jack Daniel's, I'll drink Jack Daniel's." Yes, the band members *do* influence the kids, very much so.[25]

Recalling some of the concerts of the band Journey, Dr. Taylor notes, "They use what we call an ego ramp. That's where the guy goes right into the crowd. A singer will pull out his bottle of Jack Daniel's, and the kids will pull out theirs." Nothing will stop this activity, he warns, "until someone dies." Several *have* died, and nothing has happened—yet.

Speaking from his experience supervising public safety at hundreds of events, Dr. Taylor says, "Because of the actions of a few, they have spoiled it for the general public. We're a very greedy society. We sell all the beer we want, and we don't look at what's happening because of those sales. The management just looks at the beer revenues."

Our children *can* get overloaded with the misleading messages about alcohol coming from heavy metal bands. One alcohol treatment center in Hamden, Connecticut, isolates its addicted youngsters from rock music. Opened in April 1985, the center provides a forty-five-day residential program during which the children attend school on the center's campus, go through individual and group therapy, take part in Alcoholics Anonymous and narcotics groups, exercise, and work on crafts. Though alcohol abuse is the admission ticket into the program, many of the youthful participants have used "virtually every other kind of drug," from cocaine to quaaludes, according to the director of program services at the center. Teenagers participating in the alcohol treatment program cannot listen to rock music or wear rock concert T-shirts, which the program administrators consider too closely associated with the youths' addictive behavior.[26]

ALCOHOL AND ADVERTISING

Some may feel that it's unfair to criticize musicians who promote alcohol, since alcohol is so pervasive in our society. It's true that alcohol is heavily advertised in all media, and that children are hit from all sides with messages urging them to drink. We should reconsider that practice. After all, alcohol is implicated in the loss of tens of thousands of lives annually, and causes more than $100 billion in economic damage each year. Per capita consumption of alcohol has risen nearly 50 percent in the past thirty years. Drinking and driving kill twenty-five thousand—half of all fatal automobile accidents. Alcohol-related recreational and industrial accidents claim thirty thousand more lives each year.[27]

According to statistics from the FBI and the U.S. Department of Health and Human Services, heavy drinking plays a part in 70 percent of murders, 41 percent of assaults, 53 percent of fire deaths, 50 percent of rapes, 60 percent of sex crimes against children, 60 percent of cases of child abuse, 37 percent of suicides, 55 percent of arrests, and 56 percent of fights and assaults in homes.[28] In 1984 the National PTA passed a resolution on alcohol, urging the television broadcasting industry "to eliminate unnecessary scenes depicting drinking of alcoholic beverages from TV programming when not related to the story line."[29]

Yet the alcohol industry still spends over $1 billion a year to advertise its products. This does not include the millions of dollars spent sponsoring rock concerts, intramural and Olympic athletic contests, and a variety of other college events. According to George A. Hacker, who has worked on Project SMART (Stop Marketing Alcohol on Radio and Television), "Drinking alcohol . . . is today more and more portrayed and accepted as an integral part of the 'good life.' "[30] These ads are reaching younger and younger children. Beer advertisements abound on MTV, for example, as do advertisements for wine coolers.

Since 1970, alcohol advertising budgets have jumped 490 percent on television and 300 percent on radio. "From the age of two or three, children are barraged by thousands of catchy jingles and captivating images, courtesy of the alcoholic beverage industry," says Hacker. "These ads drum home the point that good times, success, and friendships are the rewards of drinking. Such carefully crafted advertisements, along with examples set by family and peers, help mold life-long attitudes and habits."[31]

WHAT PARENTS CAN DO

As these facts show, children are at risk because of the aggressive promotion of alcohol and drugs in our society. But there are ways to respond. Understanding that parenthood is not only a precious blessing but also an awesome responsibility, I venture to suggest a few actions for parents to consider.

1. Organize a community action group of concerned parents (or join one that already exists) to urge the entertainment industry to exercise more self-restraint in the way it portrays alcohol and drug use to young people.
2. Provide a stable family relationship. In the home arena parents must help children find a meaning and set values for their lives. We ourselves have much to do with whether our children will use or misuse drugs. Ten years ago the book *Are You Driving Your Children to Drink?* described the drug abuse problem as a symptom of a more malignant underlying emotional disease caused by the disintegration of the family. Co-authors Donald A. Moses and Robert E. Burger designated unstable parent-child relation-

ships as the single most important factor leading to drug addiction.[32]

3. Remember that parents serve as role models for children. Two out of three adult Americans drink alcohol. Millions of American youth live with adults whose drinking has created problems for themselves, their families, and their employers. Many children also see a number of adults drink regularly with no apparent harm to themselves or to others.

Sometimes, the hypocrisy can be overwhelming. Some time ago a counselor received a call from a concerned mother. "I'm worried about Ginny," she told the counselor; "I think she has begun to use drugs." When the counselor asked why she suspected her daughter and what she thought she was using, the mother replied, "I think she is sneaking into my dresser drawer and getting into my Valium prescription."[33] In an imperfect world, we too must exercise personal restraint and self-discipline. We should be frank with our children about how to live well without abusing drugs of any sort.

4. Give time to your children. Families that play, work, eat, study, worship, watch television, and listen to music together have a better chance of staying together. Parents who are close to their children and show interest in them have a much greater chance of helping them avoid drug problems.

Children who seldom see their parents may well turn elsewhere for attention.

5. Establish rules but also practice democracy. We can provide an atmosphere of freedom in which our children's sense of security and self-worth will mature. Parental dictatorships only encourage revolt; a restrictive family situation can be just as dangerous as one with no rules at all. Children need to know your expectations of them as well as your concern and love for them. Consider adopting the "tough love" approach, as depicted in one episode of "The Cosby Show." In a conversation about drug use, Dr. Clifford Huxtable (Cosby) told his son Theo: "You won't use drugs in this house. When you're eighteen and out on your own, you won't use drugs. When you're seventy-five and I'm dead, you still won't use drugs!" What a great message, from one of the top-rated shows in television history!

6. Keep open two-way lines of communication. We need to talk with our children and listen to what they have to say. They need to know that we consider their opinions important. We can bridge the inevitable "generation gap" by taking the time to discuss events in their lives and ours.

7. Recognize peer pressure. Because children also spend a lot of time with their friends, peer pressure is an important force in their lives. We need to help them prepare for one of the toughest dilemmas of youth—when

to go along with the gang, and when to walk away.

8. Try not to panic about curiosity and experimentation. Adolescents in particular are curious about almost everything. Parents must not overreact when they sample, test, taste, and try things. If you think your child is experimenting with alcohol and drugs, you can talk with him or her about it—calmly, not frantically or angrily. Most children have enough sense and strength to stay out of serious trouble, but many of them will casually try an alcoholic drink or even an illegal drug.

9. Work to provide a balance of these four necessary securities: *(a) Physical security.* We should strive to give them what they need, if not always everything they want. *(b) Mental security.* We can provide an atmosphere in which our children can use their minds and expand their knowledge. We can encourage freedom of expression, questions, and discussion. We can push active pastimes like reading over passive ones like watching television. *(c) Emotional security.* We can model and teach self-control, temperance, optimism, and an enthusiastic, anticipating outlook on life. We can support youthful energies and idealism. *(d) Spiritual security.* We can work to make our homes places where family members experience an atmosphere of love that reveals the supporting spiritual nature of their lives.

10. Put love at the center of your home. We can model love, teach love, and work hard to develop a climate of understanding and love, based on mutual respect, trust, and acceptance. In such a loving home, parents and children can discuss questions and concerns about drug use and abuse, about temperance and temptation, about the rewards of responsible conduct, and together try to make the right decisions.

In this kind of home—where children are part of a loving, caring family (whether a single- or two-parent home)—parents can hope to preserve and cement the family and to teach the young to recognize the joys of living.

Rockin' and Shockin'
in the Concert Free-for-All Zone

Both reporters emerged with horror stories of a crowd that has to be frisked for firecrackers, drugs, liquor and knives; of performers who prance on stage with their backsides naked; of stabbings outside the concert hall.
—from the San Antonio Light[1]

Rock music first emerged on the national concert scene in the 1950s. Propelled by the far-reaching influence of the mass media, rock music in the decade of the eighties has become mainstream music and enjoys immense popularity. For the first time in its thirty year history, rock has widespread appeal among adults, many of whom grew up on rock and roll. In fact, we are the second rock and roll generation of parents—parents who understand rock and its appeal for our own children. We are tolerant and liberal in our attitudes toward this music, which has always been regarded as the particular domain of rebellious youth.

THE POSITIVE SIDE

In recent years we have witnessed some marvelous examples of how mainstream rock and roll and its public performance can be utilized for good. Irish rock musician Bob Geldof, for example, organized the Live Aid concert to raise money for African famine relief. He influenced American rock stars to come together to record "We Are the World."

Written by Lionel Ritchie and Michael Jackson, the song aimed at raising awareness about the famine and money to assist its victims. The broadcast of the Live Aid concert generated pledges totalling $70 million.[2] An estimated 40 million Americans saw ABC's three-hour prime-time show; the simultaneous MTV broadcast reached 27.3 million homes.[3] The concert was also beamed via satellite into 152 countries where as many as 1.5 billion people could have seen it.[4]

Other philanthropic concerts raised money for hunger here in the U.S. (Band Aid), the farm crisis (Farm Aid), and human rights (Conspiracy of Hope). While rock and roll performers obviously cannot participate in such benevolent projects every month, the public would welcome more such expressions of social responsibility. Such events are terrific for our spirits. They touch us all; they make us proud of rock and roll and, as fans and consumers of music, proud to share in a noble cooperative effort. In a sense, Live Aid returned us to an earlier era, a time when many of us felt that music brought our generation together.

Rock and roll is a loud, raucous, exuberant, proud celebration of life and love, conquests and heartaches. Rock concerts have always primarily been a gathering of people who wanted to have a good time, to affirm their uniqueness in the world, and for a few brief hours, to be carefree.

A LEAK IN THE ROCK UNDERGROUND

While many rock concerts are nothing to worry about, the advent of punk and heavy metal music has changed the ambience of many local concert halls. Some newer concert acts are violent, sexually explicit, vulgar, and profane. Rock concerts are singular in one important regard: In almost all other entertainment media, vulgar and violent stage acts are segregated from the mainstream, and certainly from children.

Yet songs and stage performances today often deal with such unconventional subjects as sadism and masochism—once limited to an underground market. Like a toxic waste dump, this hidden subculture has begun poisoning mainstream rock. Some heavy metal rock performers have expressly designed their concerts to display depraved, violent behavior that stimulates and inflames hostile emotions. In fact, some rock concerts include such explicit content that, were they movies, they would certainly be rated X or at least R for their language, lewdness, or violence. Yet many young children attend these concerts. They are promoted by local radio stations which give away tickets and backstage passes. Thousands of parents ferry their youngsters—some nine, ten, and eleven years of age—to concert arenas, often with no idea what these children may hear or see there: profanities, details of sexual encounters, descriptions of the thrills of drinking and taking dope. The messages are all the more powerful because they come from stars whom many kids worship. Since outrageous showmanship substitutes for musical talent for many of these idolized groups, our concert-going children may well see performances involving simulated sexual acts or extreme violence.

Most of the worst excesses occur at heavy metal concerts; this kind of trouble just doesn't seem to occur at symphony concerts, jazz festivals, or classical quartet performances. Fights do sometimes break out at country music concerts when fans drink too much. Trouble can also occur at major sporting events, or at any large public gathering, for that matter. But a pattern of increasing violence, which seems to accelerate with the increasingly aggressive and sexually explicit behavior of the performers, can be detected in the reported incidents of violence and drug abuse at rock concerts.

● Iron Maiden, a heavy metal group popular with adolescents, put on a concert in Buffalo, New York, during which its lead singer, Bruce Dickinson, allegedly stripped a woman of the top part of her outfit, against her will. She filed a $250,000 suit against him.[5]

● Angus Young of AC/DC reportedly pulls his pants down to shock his young audiences.[6]

● To an audience of youngsters between twelve and seventeen, Vince Neil of Mötley Crüe reportedly shouted, "We're on a never ending search for the best piece of [deleted word] in the world. . . . Who is the best [deleted word] in Memphis?"[7] (Brackets indicate deletions present in original material.) This stage show really shouldn't shock us, when we realize that this band's lyrics reek with sexual references, such as, "Ninety thousand screaming watts/Honey dripping from her pot. . . ./Pleasure victim, who's next to fall/The question is will you please us all tonight?"[8]

● The *Denver Post* reported that at the Brendon Byrne Arena in New Jersey, rock star Billy Idol stood at the edge of the stage and encouraged two young girls to fondle him.[9]

● The *San Antonio Light* reported of W.A.S.P. in concert:

> "I wanna know how many of you f[uck]ers are here tonight looking for a little p[uss]y?" the band's lead singer shouts. . . . Looking at all these beautiful women, I'm getting pretty *hot*. And when you get hot, I hope you take care of the situation the same way I do. I like to *f[uck] on the beach!!* And when you f[uck] on the beach, there's only one way to do it—*like an animaaaaallllllll!!*[10]

And that is only the introduction to a song.

These groups wouldn't be allowed to get away with such vulgarity if the promoters and the city or county councils who have jurisdiction over concert facilities got together and required them to clean up their acts. But rock groups' performances receive support from adults in the business world—including promoters, record company executives, and even some city government officials.

The broadcasting industry has also frequently abetted the problems. Many local radio stations hawk the bands coming to town, without any regard for the nature of their performances, offer contests or develop trivia questions to help promote attendance, and give out prizes of free tickets to the concerts or maybe even backstage passes to kids of any age. Who wouldn't like to go backstage to meet James Taylor, Whitney Houston, or other fine stars? But there's a world of difference between backstage introductions to mainline artists and the backstage activities of the punk and metal groups.

147

CAPITALIZING ON THE CULT OF VIOLENCE

By far, the worst concert excesses of the "concept" acts involve violence. In fact, some groups have capitalized on the cult of violence (á la *Rambo* or *The Texas Chainsaw Massacre*), promoting themselves by using graphic, simulated violence in their stage acts. For instance, pictures and posters show Blackie Lawless of W.A.S.P. drinking "blood" out of a human skull, an act he has performed on stage. The stage shows of some bands include reproductions of torture racks, skulls, and ghouls—images of death and destruction that make Dante's description of hell look like a nursery school playground. Using these visual props, the stars simulate all kinds of acts of violence, almost always perpetrated against women.

• Past performances of the group W.A.S.P. have included simulated acts of extreme violence against half-nude women involving torture racks, attacks with knives and circular saw blades, and of course, much fake blood.

• A videocassette tape of a concert by the band Lizzy Borden shows one of the band members putting a woman into a long box and then chopping down into the box with an ax. He fills his mouth with the "blood" that spurts into the air and spits it out at the audience.[11]

• Alice Cooper, now engaged in a performing comeback, uses a guillotine to sever the head of a mannequin on stage. Says Cooper: "It's more anatomically correct than it used to be. I advise anybody in the first few rows to wear blood bibs or raincoats."[12]

Does any of this violence have an effect on the

kids? "Do you ever have second thoughts about your influence on teen-agers?" a magazine writer asked Nikki Sixx. "No," the heavy metal rocker replied, "I think we have a positive message. It's very much an American message: Live free, express yourself, and it's up to the youth to change the world. And also, just have a good time."[13]

BEGETTING MORE VIOLENCE

While the concerts of many rock performers do provide fun and wholesome entertainment, in the last few years newspapers have carried more and more stories about violence occurring among and against concertgoers themselves, especially at heavy metal rock concerts. Undeniably, rock concerts have changed, and some of them now clearly pose potential public health hazards.

Professor Carl Taylor, president of the Detroit security company that has worked with many traveling rock shows, worries about the fact that parents do not know what goes on at some concerts. "A lot of parents are basing their decisions on the past, when they were teens," he notes. "They don't realize how much things have changed."[14]

In the days of Elvis Presley and the Beatles' concerts, Dr. Taylor points out, there was "controlled frenzy, but there was no socking someone in the mouth." Dr. Taylor thinks that the image of the band dictates the behavior of its audience. "It sets the standard," he asserts. "The kids look up to these bands."[15]

Large numbers of young people are high on drugs or intoxicated at these concerts. Not all the predators are on the stage. Large concerts attract some who would take advantage of the young, the inexperienced, the unprotected, the unsuspecting. Many preteens and adolescents become victims in more than one way.

Here is just a sampling of the violence associated with rock concerts, which has been escalating over the past eight years. And keep in mind that, as Dr. Taylor warns, most crimes and sexual abuses at concerts go unreported because the young people are too scared to go to the authorities, since they are usually high or drunk themselves.

● In 1979, eleven young people were killed while waiting to enter a concert given by the English band the Who, in Cincinnati. In response to that tragedy, Cincinnati outlawed the practice of "festival seating," in which seating is not assigned but rather determined by one's position in the waiting line.[16]

● In 1981, there were two reported rapes connected to rock concerts. One was in Chicago,[17] the other in the Superdome parking lot in New Orleans.[18]

● In 1983, roving bands of youths attacked and harassed fans leaving the Diana Ross concert in New York's Central Park.[19]

● On May 24, 1984, in Louisiana, there was an attempted rape by two seventeen-year-old boys of two girls, fourteen and sixteen years old, in the University of New Orleans Lakefront Arena.[20]

● In 1985 in Phoenix, Arizona, one drug-related death and three stabbings took place at a rock concert at the Compton Terrace Pavilion.[21] In New York City, stabbings and fights resulted in eighteen arrests after a concert by the rap groups Run D.M.C. and the Fat Boys.[22] In Wisconsin, the *Milwaukee Journal* reported that a sixteen-year-old boy was accused of a rape that occurred on the floor during a Mötley Crüe concert at that city's arena.[23] Later that year, a seventeen-year-old girl was raped during a concert in Los Angeles featuring the group "X."[24]

In 1986, the violence became more frequent and severe:

• On May 18, in Tacoma, Washington, during a Judas Priest concert at the Tacoma Dome, a nineteen-year-old man was killed in a knife attack; the assailant's sixteen-year-old girlfriend was also stabbed in the incident.[25]

• On May 29, in Kalamazoo, Michigan, a woman was raped near Wings Stadium after attending a Judas Priest concert. A hit-and-run accident killed an eighteen-year-old boy at a nearby intersection, and three concert-goers were injured, two seriously, in a separate automobile accident.[26]

• On June 9, in New York City, following a concert by New Edition at Madison Square Garden, gangs of marauding youth robbed and mugged fans during a two-hour crime spree that resulted in twelve injuries and twenty-six arrests of persons ranging in age from thirteen to twenty-eight, including one person armed with a gun.[27]

• On June 14, in Long Beach, California, twenty-two-year-old John Loftus fell to his death from the bleachers during an Ozzy Osbourne concert. Three other persons had to be hospitalized, two boys in serious condition with skull fractures. Ten people received treatment for injuries at a local hospital; a hospital spokeswoman said all the injuries had occurred in the vicinity of the concert.[28]

• On June 28, in Pittsburgh, Pennsylvania, after a concert at the Civic Arena by rap artists L. L. Cool J and Run D.M.C., hundreds of young people roamed downtown streets, where they attacked innocent people and vandalized property.[29] The members of Run D.M.C. argue that their lyrics are positive and that they have been unfairly accused of promoting violence. Nevertheless, twenty-two persons were injured, four seriously, at the Pittsburgh concert; one had a skull fracture. Police arrested twenty-five people, including nine juveniles, one of whom was eleven years old. The director of public safety for Pittsburgh said that there was "no doubt" that drugs, alcohol, and violent lyrics contributed to the rampage of violence. "There's no question in my mind [that it] was drug- and alcohol-related," the city's public health director stated. He stressed that parents need to know what's happening at concerts: "The lyrics in the songs are provocative and pornographic. They incite violence."[30] As a result of the violence, the mayor of Pittsburgh threatened to set a moratorium or to ban some rock concerts to prevent further occurrences of crime sprees by fans.[31]

• On August 15, a fan was so severely beaten at a Run D.M.C. concert in Fresno, California, that he later died.[32] Two days later, fifteen fans were sent to hospitals following the outbreak of fighting at a Run D.M.C. concert in Long Beach.[33]

• The December 6, 1986, issue of *Billboard* reported a $5 million lawsuit filed against the band Aerosmith by a woman who was hit in the face during one of their concerts. She was knocked unconscious and suffered a broken nose. The suit claims that the woman's injuries were a direct consequence of the group's purposefully communicated image, on stage and in their recordings, of "encouraging violence and other unlawful and outrageous acts." The song "My Fist in Your Face" has been specifically cited in the lawsuit.[34]

PROTECTING CHILDREN

For the sake of our children, we parents should become more aware of what goes on at rock concerts. Depending on their ages, we should go with our younger children to concerts; we should provide clear guidelines and safety rules to those teens we are not going to accompany to the concert center. We must get at least rudimentary information about the nature of the band performing and decide if it will provide proper entertainment for our children. (To its credit, Twisted Sister has put a warning about profane language in at least some of their concert ads.) We ought to be able to obtain this information from the promoters of the concert; in fact, the community should pressure promoters to routinely provide the public with such information. Until and unless such information becomes readily available, we will have to look to the newspapers that carry concert advertisements, to the radio stations promoting a concert, and to knowledgeable record store personnel who might be willing to respond to inquiries.

Unless we live in San Antonio, Texas, or in some

other city whose civic and political leaders have been stirred to action, we will be very much alone as we seek this kind of information. However, we should express our desire for more information about concerts from their commercial sponsors and from the owners of the facilities where the bands play. Such consumer demands are one of the only ways we can get some action in the public interest. Where municipal authorities control the arena, citizens' political action may be effective in producing information about performances.

Dr. Taylor thinks that concerts should be rated like movies and the ratings advertised in the local media. He points to the Eddie Murphy comedy shows for which the advertisements state that no one under eighteen should come without a parent. From his years of experience working with rock concerts and studying human behavior in the concert arena, as well as from his role as a university professor, Dr. Taylor is in a unique position to make recommendations to parents on dealing with rock concerts. With his permission, I would like to mention some suggestions from his handbook, *Rock Concerts: A Parent's Guide.*[35]

GUIDELINES FOR ROCK CONCERTS

Concerned parents should take a number of steps to ensure the safety of their children at rock concerts. If we plan to drop preteens off, even to meet with a group, and pick them up after the concert, we should think about how well they could handle all of the possibilities.

Dr. Taylor advises that an adult should accompany

most young teens to concerts. Older teens (sixteen and up) can go with a group of friends. When we go with children, we should not send them to the rest rooms or concession stands unescorted. "Many times teenagers are harassed and sold anything one can imagine by opportunists," Dr. Taylor states, "especially in populated areas like restrooms and concession stands."[36]

"A teenager should never drive to a concert alone." If the facility is located in the city, teenage drivers should park in the concert parking lot or as close to the arena as possible. He or she should "never park in a deserted area." Teens shouldn't park far away from the concert center, Dr. Taylor warns, because there is a risk of car theft, robbery, and rape.[37]

We should tell teens not to wear expensive-looking jewelry to the concert. "Leave the flash at home to avoid becoming a target for muggers and thieves," Dr. Taylor suggests.[38]

All girls should go to a concert in groups of at least four, Dr. Taylor advises, and during the concert none of the girls should go to the rest room by herself.[39]

We should warn children of the fire hazards of holding lighted butane lighters aloft to signal approval of a performance.[40] Many fans also like to throw firecrackers into the audience.

We need to warn our children that many concerts are rife with people high on alcohol and drugs, and with others selling drugs. We need to give them guidance on how to handle these temptations, as well as on the dangers posed by drunken fellow concert-goers. Alcohol and drugs often play a significant part in the accidents that happen at concerts.

How can the excesses, the indecencies, and the violence of some rock concerts which I have cited in this chapter be properly handled? First, it is not a problem for the federal government to control. It is a local problem subject to regulation by the local community, if the public's health and safety is involved. Within those limits, the community itself can decide what will be allowed to go on at public concerts—usually held in publicly owned buildings.

But most important of all, parents should take a close look at the way *some* of today's rock performers relate to their young audiences. All parents should resolve to take a stand to protect their children, and explain this to them. We may need to attend concerts with our children, or just have the conviction and simple courage to sometimes say, "No, you can't go." Furthermore, we should share our concerns with other parents so that we can support each other and not fight a lonely struggle. In short, we really need to wake up to some of the new and frightening realities of rock concerts, because much of what goes on at too many concerts is not only shocking, but dangerous.

Parenting in an Explicit Society

*There's nothing you can do that can't be done. . . ./All you
need is love.*
— "All You Need Is Love," by the Beatles[1]

National groups like the PMRC and the American
Academy of Pediatrics (with whom the PMRC has
recently formed a coalition) will keep fighting to
encourage corporations to be responsible for their
products and to help local communities develop
constructive approaches to this problem. But perhaps
most important, parents are waking up to the need to
address these issues within the family. Over the past
two years of working on this problem, I have met
thousands of such concerned parents, and I am
convinced that they can reassert a more responsible
standard for public values. This generation of parents
has a special duty to establish a moral imperative for
our children—to reject violence in favor of hope and
love; to reject death and destruction in favor of life; to
reject exploitation in favor of nurture.

The art of parenting should be approached with the
same conviction and dedication as a professional
career. Don't underestimate the importance of your
imagination and inventiveness just because parenting involves the home, children, and twenty-four-
hour relationships.

The importance of communication cannot be over-emphasized. Concert promoters, law enforcement officials, and teachers alike stress the value of keeping open the lines of communication with children, and of listening to their concerns as well as expressing your own. Much more can be accomplished through your willingness to communicate openly than by laying down and inflexibly enforcing a lot of misunderstood rules, then trying to justify them with a "Because I said so!" Because children learn by example, you can teach them how to communicate by doing a credible job of it yourself.

Rules and limits are more important than a lot of parents realize. I learned that simple but important lesson myself with my first child, who was overly demanding and had me wrapped around her finger at two years of age. My mother gently and wisely pointed out to me that to set limits and stick to them would improve the relationship and provide some relief to this curious and testing little person. It did, and I have tried to remember that lesson and apply it accordingly.

PARENTAL SOLIDARITY

Many homes have only one parent, who more than likely works, or two parents who are both working. The stresses and strains these parents face in raising children and balancing jobs and other pressures require creative solutions. With organization, creativity, and planning, you can establish a structure and rules that will keep your family running smoothly. If, as working parents, you don't have as much time to devote to your home and children as you would like to have, you can still help to shape your children by imparting values, planning activities, and setting limits.

Networking with other parents in the neighborhood is an invaluable tool for this. Networks and parent peer groups can be set up through schools, churches and synagogues, community centers, and neighborhoods. In many such groups, parents meet for a few hours a month to discuss common goals and problems. Networking can deal with such issues as telephone hours, dating, R-rated movies, videotape rental policies, and peer pressure. Parental solidarity is one way to keep kids within bounds. Even if various sets of parents privately disagree, they can respect each other's wishes and not show an R-rated movie to a neighbor's thirteen-year-old if the visiting child's parents would object. That kind of care should become part of "high tech" hospitality.

Give your child clear guidelines on what to do if R-rated videos or other adult materials are brought out at a slumber party. You can always make some exceptions, but it helps the child to know what to expect, even though he or she may protest. I have taken my twelve-year-old to a good, but R rated, movie, because the rating in that case was primarily for language and I was confident she could handle it. She can see that I am somewhat flexible and reasonable, even though she knows how strongly I feel and why. The parent who cares will impose restrictions on his or her children. Those who don't, won't.

Below are some ways for parents to work together in a community.

PARENTS IN THE COMMUNITY

1. To reiterate, get together with your child's friends' parents, let them know how you feel, and get their perspective. Build parental solidarity. You won't get everyone to agree, but you might be surprised at the number of other parents who feel as you do yet don't know what to do about a seemingly overwhelming problem. Network with other parents to present kids with a unified front.

   This is especially important now, with so much variety in home entertainment available, some of it completely inappropriate for children to view. Your child may visit in a home that receives the Exstasy hard-core pornography channel, or other cable channels with horribly violent movies. Find out if the parents in that home lock such channels out, or have any method to restrict their availability to children.

2. Share your concerns about concert attendance with other parents, and figure out rules behind which you can all unite. It makes life easier for everyone.

3. Participate in and help to organize community action or awareness groups and choose what kind of action is most needed in your community. Work through the local PTA or civic groups. Such groups might:
   —Check local record stores to see if records and tapes carry essential consumer infor-

mation on their contents. If a violent or pornographic album is prominently displayed, objections should be voiced to the store manager and store owner. Ask for more sensitive treatment of that type of product. After all, magazines of that nature are usually kept under cover or behind the counter; why should records be treated any differently, if their contents are essentially the same?

—Campaign for community ordinances to regulate young people's access to explicit rock music concerts and what is allowed to occur at them. Petition the city government to require an adequate number of security guards so that young concert-goers will be protected.

4. Monitor local television programming and complain to the local station manager and owner about offensive shows. File a copy of the complaint with the Federal Communications Commission in Washington. If there is no response, create a coalition of groups, go to the sponsors who buy the advertising, and voice the group's concerns to them. If all else fails, you might consider organizing a consumer boycott. It is a legal and frequently effective technique for applying community pressure. Constitutional lawyers agree that there is no First Amendment problem with a properly handled, non-government-related boycott. But it should be used carefully and only as a last resort.

5. Monitor local radio and television broadcasts. If offensive material is aired, write down the objectionable words, songs, or scenes; the name and date of the program; and its commercial sponsors. Send a letter of protest to the local station manager and the program's sponsors, giving specific details of objectionble material. If you have complaints about socially unacceptable programming on cable television, such as MTV or other music video programs, write to the executive director of the National Cable Television Association or the president of MTV, or both.

6. File petitions with the Federal Communications Commission in Washington to request inquiries into the license renewals of television and radio stations that violate the public interest by broadcasting excessively violent movies and shows.

7. Petition cable companies to place violent R- and X-rated films on a separate channel and to make the lockout feature available on all channel-switching devices provided to subscribers. If they don't do these two things, cancel your subscription, and let them know why.

8. Be sure that video rental stores do not rent adult videos to persons under seventeen. Let the owner and manager know that you want this age limit enforced, and that you want them to provide consumer information on the tapes.

9. Write the companies, be they movie or record, that produce violent or sexually explicit entertainment. You don't have to watch it, but you should let producers know how you feel about the excesses they are promoting to society.

10. Write the president of the Recording Industry Association of America (RIAA), which represents 85 percent of the recording industry, if you wish to protest a record album, its contents, or its jacket. Make sure you clearly identify the band, the album, and when necessary, the song. State your objection in precise terms.

   When writing broadcasters and the RIAA, always send copies of your correspondence to the Federal Communications Commission, the National Association of Broadcasters, and to your elected representatives at both the state and national level. Their addresses may be found in the Media Action and Resource Agency Directory in Appendix B.

11. Media education begins in the home. Spend time with your child listening to and discussing music, or viewing television programs and videocassettes. Set some common sense rules about what your children can and cannot listen to and watch, and above all, enforce them!

12. To stop direct mail porn advertisements, go to your local post office and file an "Application for Listing Pursuant to 39 USC

3010." This procedure allows you to remove yourself and members of your family from mailing lists used by distributors of sexually oriented advertisements. If the distributors ignore this legal request that you stop receiving this kind of material in the mail you can file a formal complaint with the United States Postal Service. Violators of this provision can be subject to both civil and criminal legal action by the U.S. Government.

Many argue that it is not the job of the entertainment industry to lead us to a higher spiritual or intellectual plane. It is fortunate that it often does so, and I applaud it when it does. But we must also criticize it for its all too frequent excesses. Of course, we all share some responsibity for the degeneration of the quality of media offerings. We have been complacent. The market carries only what consumers buy. But if we educate ourselves and communicate our concerns to the entertainment industry, we can bring to bear our powerful consumer influence for more socially responsible media programming. Only by rejecting the status quo will we create a market for more positive themes. It's a big job, but we can do it. We can make a difference.

Conclusion

The fundamental problem I have outlined in this book is one of excess. Sexually explicit, violent, destructive entertainment is being aggressively marketed to an audience that includes preteens, young teens, and older adolescents, by commercial interests who have demonstrated an astounding lack of accountability for their actions.

Excessive and explicit violence is promoted in many entertainment offerings, even though our country is already one of the most crime-ridden in the developed world. American men have a one in one hundred chance of being murdered at some time in their lives. The risk is twice that for non-whites. Shouldn't those figures make us think twice about glorifying murder and mayhem?

Our teenage suicide rate has increased 300 percent since 1950. Thirteen teens kill themselves each day, five thousand each year. Yet some musicians and record companies continue to produce songs that glorify suicide, despite scientific evidence that some teenagers are prone to imitate suicides they hear about in the media.

Teen pregnancy is an epidemic in America. Each year, over one million teens get pregnant—the highest rate in the developed world. Yet the entertainment industry goes on saturating the teen market with increasingly explicit sexual themes. Sex has become little more than a commodity, peddled to young people by advertisers and record companies.

Drugs and alcohol claim more young victims every day. Yet some rock stars flaunt drugs and drinking in their stage acts and public interviews. According to *Parade Magazine*, in the past five years at least sixty major motion pictures, many of them favorites with youngsters, included scenes showing recreational drug use.[1]

But there are ways to fight back. Many parents and concerned citizens are doing just that. We in the PMRC have met these people in our travels to communities all over this country. Americans are beginning to open their eyes and ears.

Thankfully, some in the music industry are also waking up. Columbia Records just canceled a deal to distribute Slayer's latest album, called *Reign in Blood*, which includes sickening references to the infamous Nazi murderer Doctor Josef Mengele.[2] George David Weiss, president of the Songwriters Guild of America, has called on artists to be more responsible and to exercise self-restraint in lyrics and videos.[3]

Legendary singer and Motown great Smokey Robinson has denounced "auditory pornography" and has urged artists to be more sensitive to young fans. His song "Be Kind to the Growing Mind" reflects his strong conviction that porn rock is harmful to children of all ages.

Other talented stars have helped make a difference. Paul McCartney, formerly of the Beatles, has acknowledged the need for the PMRC's work. He says things are getting farther and farther out and it's good for somebody to keep an eye on them.[4] The original funding for the PMRC came from the generous and committed Mike Love of the popular band, the Beach Boys. He, too, is disturbed by the entertainment industry's penchant for the violent and explicit.

Finally, through the efforts of enlightened music industry executives like our industry ally, it may be possible to halt the moral and artistic decline of much American entertainment. Parents everywhere owe them many thanks.

It's not easy being a parent these days. It's even tougher being a kid. Perhaps together we can help our society grow up.

Appendix A

TAKING ACTION: A TALE OF TWO CITIES

At the grass-roots level, citizens' groups are beginning to form all over the country to demand that the youth entertainment industry exercise some self-restraint and show some responsibility, especially in regard to public rock concerts. Two communities that have taken the lead in this effort are Memphis, Tennessee, and San Antonio, Texas.

MEMPHIS

Nowhere has a community response to this challenge been greater or more committed than in Memphis, Tennessee. I presented the PMRC slide show and talked about music lyrics to the members of the Memphis Junior League in January 1986. The enthusiastic response of these concerned women resulted in an invitation to address the Memphis Kiwanis Club in April, where the response of the fathers, grandfathers, and other concerned men in the audience was again overwhelming. The coalition immediately elected a steering committee to direct the ensuing citizen activism. Several members of the Junior League, the president of the Kiwanis Club and representatives from the Rotary Club, Memphis State University, the chief of police, the Center City Commission, and others joined together to organize a group called Community Awareness of Music and Entertainment Content Coalition (CAMEC), in the spring of 1986. This citizens' coalition represents the first time in Memphis' history that these civic groups have worked together closely on one project.

The purpose of CAMEC is to "promote public awareness of the character and content of entertainment for youth, and to encourage enforcement of existing laws at entertainment facilities." The organizers of CAMEC stress that the coalition's sole purpose is public education, and emphasize avoidance of censorship. "We absolutely don't want to be in a boycott or censorship mode," one Kiwanis member said.

CAMEC's specific areas of concern are:
1. To educate the community and promote coalition building. They set a goal of presenting the PMRC slide show statewide to two hundred community groups by the end of 1987.
2. To make sure that existing laws governing alcohol and drug use at local concerts are enforced, through adult monitoring.
3. To explore the possibility of separating MTV from the local basic cable package so subscribers can choose whether to have it or not.

4. To urge the cable company to place R-rated movies containing scenes of violence and sex on a separate pay channel.
5. To monitor television and radio for explicit violence and sex and to let stations and advertisers know of any excesses.

Any citizen group would do well to follow the Memphis organization's blueprint. CAMEC began by holding organizational meetings to decide how they wanted to proceed and to clearly define their purpose, goals, and objectives. They proceeded with participation and advice from the Tennessee state attorney general, the city attorney, a city council representative, a state senator, and the chief of police. The group hired a full-time staff person to coordinate their efforts. They acquired a central phone number and address and advertised it to the community. Then they obtained a copy of the PMRC slide show for duplication and distribution.

Now CAMEC is developing a handbook of methods and programs which will eventually be distributed by the national offices of CAMEC's participating organizations. Carrying out these ambitious objectives involves analyzing and documenting the start-up procedures that CAMEC used in Memphis. The group has also developed a statewide network to enlarge the effort by contacting groups with already existing chapters throughout the state.

CAMEC has become an ideal model of how to build a successful coalition. The group offered member organizations start-up assistance and information, contacted influential people in towns that don't have local chapters of national organizations, and established a statewide newsletter that reports on the activities of its constituent groups. The individuals involved in CAMEC mean business, and are bringing results.

SAN ANTONIO

In November 1985, with the courageous leadership of Mayor Henry Cisneros, the City Council of San Antonio, Texas, passed and signed into law the first ordinance restricting unaccompanied minors from attending lewd and violent rock concerts. The ordinance simply states that no child under thirteen can attend an obscene concert unless accompanied by a parent or guardian. Since promoters and artists themselves were doing nothing to address the problem of young children attending raunchy shows, the city government decided to act on its own. San Antonio showed the rest of the nation what caring citizens can accomplish.

In the summer of 1985, several parents' groups in San Antonio brought their concerns before the city council and urged them to take action to deal with heavy metal concerts—at least those showing at city-owned facilities. Bobbie Mueller, president of Community Families in Action, a group concerned about teenage drug abuse, attended a concert where she observed widespread drug use among young teens. She was shocked, and went before the city council the next day to share her concern.

Mueller recommends this route to other concerned parents. It is important to inform city councils of your interest, she says, so that you can make it clear that you intend to get more parents involved.

Representatives of the community network of parents' groups, including the local PTA unit president, persuaded the city council to pass an ordinance regulating attendance at explicit public performances, which included rock concerts. More important, they succeeded in raising the public's and the public officials' awareness about music issues. The council passed an ordinance in September of 1985 banning smoking at city concert halls. It banned cigar, cigarette, and pipe smoking, except in the rest rooms. In November, the council went further, voting to restrict admission to obscene performances for children thirteen and under, unless they are accompanied by a parent or legal guardian. "We have been respectful of the First Amendment," Mayor Cisneros argued.[1]

The parents' groups were opposed by Jack Orbin, president of Stone City Attractions, Inc., which promotes shows in Texas, Oklahoma, Louisiana, and New Mexico, and by the Texas American Civil Liberties Union. In fairness to Mr. Orbin, while he was opposed to passage of the ordinance, he is a father himself and demonstrated some concern about the issue raised.

During the debate on a related San Antonio ordinance, the city hired a psychiatrist, Dr. Robert Demski, to help determine the age at which children become vulnerable to explicit messages in hard rock. Dr. Demski said that he would support a rating system for rock concerts similar to that used for motion pictures. He added that children from about ages eleven to fourteen should not be allowed into some rock concerts unless accompanied by an adult.[2]

"Most rock is OK," Dr. Demski noted. "The part that we're concerned with is the glorification of [suicide, drug and alcohol abuse, and] degrading sex."[3] These kinds of themes are dangerous to children who are depressed or emotionally disturbed. Taking those and other conclusions into account, the San Antonio City Council developed and approved the new ordinance on rock concerts.

A year later, I asked Mrs. Mueller about her reaction to the ordinance. "The ordinance is working well," she told me. "It has cleaned up the stage shows. I am a little disappointed in the way the smoking ordinance is being enforced. There could be more diligence from the police. But it has definitely improved things. We have more parents going to concerts now. It has been the most marvelous improvement in our area because that's the way to change things—to get parents involved! We have awakened the whole community to the negativism of some of the concerts."[4]

Both San Antonio and Memphis have led the way.

Appendix B

Media Action and Resource Agency Directory

GOVERNMENT AND INDUSTRY INFORMATION RESOURCES

Federal Communications Commission
Chief of Complaints
Mass Media Bureau
1919 M Street, NW
Washington, DC 20554

Music Television (MTV)
President
1775 Broadway
New York, NY 10019

National Association of Broadcasters
Mr. Eddie Fritts, President
  & Chief Executive Officer
1771 N Street, NW
Washington, DC 20036

National Association of Independent Record Distributors and Manufacturers
Ms. Holly Cass, Executive Director
6935 Airport Highway Lane
Pennsauken, NJ 08109
(609) 665-8085

National Cable Television Association
Mr. Jim Mooney, Executive Director
1724 Massachusetts Avenue, NW
Washington, DC 20036

Recording Industry Association of America
Mr. Jay Berman, President
1020 19th Street, NW, Suite 200
Washington, DC 20036

United States Representative
The Honorable (Name of your representative)
U.S. House of Representatives
Washington, DC 20515

United States Senator
The Honorable (Name of your senators)
U.S. Senate
Washington, DC 20510

NETWORKS

American Broadcasting Company
Audience Information
1330 Avenue of the Americas
New York, NY 10019
(212) 887-7777

Christian Broadcasting Network
CBN Center
Virginia Beach, VA 23463
(804) 424-7777

Columbia Broadcasting System
Entertainment Division
51 West 52nd Street
New York, NY 10019
(212) 975-4321

National Broadcasting Company
Audience Services
30 Rockefeller Plaza
New York, NY 10020
(212) 664-4444

Public Broadcasting Service
1320 Braddock Place
Alexandria, VA 22314
(703) 739-5000

Trinity Broadcasting Network
Box A
Santa Ana, CA 92711
(404) 827-1500

Turner Broadcasting System
1050 Techwood Drive, NW
Atlanta, GA 30318
(404) 827-1500

ROCK MUSIC AND CONCERTS

American Academy of Pediatrics
141 Northwest Point Boulevard
P. O. Box 927
Elk Grove Village, IL 60009-0927
(312) 228-5005

Back in Control Center
1234 W. Chapman, Suite 203
Orange, CA 92668
(714) 538-2563

A family training center run by former probation officers, set up to help troubled kids who are deeply involved with punk rock or heavy metal.

Community Awareness of Music and Entertainment
    Content
Kiwanis Club of Memphis
149 Union Avenue
Memphis, TN 38103
(901) 526-1818

A model for coalition efforts within local communities; has sought "to establish a community education program on today's entertainment content by means of a coalition of national and local organizations in Memphis, Tennessee."

Cornerstone Media, Inc.
P.O. Box 6236
Santa Rosa, CA 95406
(707) 542-8273

Music Research Institute
3400 Eleventh Street
San Pablo, CA 94806
(415) 236-3820

National PTA
700 North Rush Street
Chicago, IL 60611-1571
(312) 787-0977

Provides resource material for parents on a variety of subjects, such as leadership and legislation, drug and alcohol concerns, education, health, safety, parenting, television, and other media. Develops programs for use by local chapters of the PTA. One recently developed program is a parenting skills kit; "Parenting: The Underdeveloped Skill" includes discussion of diet, hygiene, physical fitness, sex, teen stressors, building self-esteem, and many other topics of concern to parents and children. It is available through the National PTA.

Parents' Music Resource Center
Ms. Jennie Norwood, Executive Director
1500 Arlington Boulevard
Suite 300
Arlington, VA 22209
(703) 527-9466

Has led the effort, in cooperation with the National PTA, to encourage responsibility and self-restraint in the recording industry. Available PMRC resources include:

Rise to the Challenge—twenty-minute videocassette (VHS) produced by the PMRC and Teen Vision, that examines today's popular music and gives examples of album covers, song lyrics, and concerts depicting violence, drug use, and explicit sex. Parents advised that some examples shown may not be appropriate for their children. $39.00 plus $2.50 postage and handling. Also available in 16 mm; call for information.

Let's Talk Rock: A Parent's Primer—handbook filled with advice from experts on how to deal with teenage drug use, rock concerts, teenage suicide, and more. $2.50; designed to accompany the above videocassette.

Rock Music Report—thirty-minute audiocassette filled with examples of today's music and quotes from magazines, artists, and industry personnel. $5.00.

Press Kit—complete package of information including surveys, studies, articles, quotes, sample lyrics, news releases, and a complete history of the PMRC from its beginnings in 1985 to the present. $10.00.

Community Families in Action
Post Office Box 6724
San Antonio, TX 78209
(512) 824-7823

An affiliate of Parents for Drug Free Youth; sponsored the model legislation on rock concerts passed by the San Antonio City Council.

Dr. Carl Spencer Taylor
P.O. Box 1704
East Lansing, MI 48823

Author of *Rock Concerts: A Parent's Guide,* also a university professor and president of a company that specializes in rock concert security.

THE MEDIA AND MEDIA VIOLENCE

The organizations listed under rock music and rock concerts will have numerous resources for dealing with violence in the media. However, the premier organization for information on media violence is:

National Coalition on Television Violence
P.O. Box 2157
Champaign, IL 61820
(217) 384-1920
    or
144 East End Avenue
New York, NY 10128
(212) 535-7275

Has done research on a wide variety of media and products—television, music, music videos, war toys—that glorify violence. Besides its national office, it has a New York office.

Action for Children's Television
20 University Road
Cambridge, MA 02138
(617) 876-6620

A nonprofit child advocacy organization working to improve children's television. A terrific group. Publishes *The TV-Smart Book for Kids*—a fun-filled educational tool for children to help them manage their television habits, with puzzles, games, activities, and pictures, organized around a colorful fill-in calendar that can be started any month of the year. Includes a special booklet for parents. $6.95.

Media Action Research Center (MARC)
475 Riverside Drive
Suite 1370
New York, NY 10115
(212) 865-6690

A nonprofit educational organization formed to research the impact of television on viewers and to create resources that would explore the media's influence on society.

A key resource published by MARC, in cooperation with thirteen religious groups, is *On Media & Values*, produced four times a year "as a forum to stimulate creative thinking about values in the media age." *On Media & Values*, 1962 S. Shenandoah, Los Angeles, CA 90034, (213) 559-2944. Subscription price: $12 per year.

Morality in Media, Inc.
475 Riverside Drive
New York, NY 10115
(212) 870-3222

MAJOR RECORDING COMPANIES

Capitol Records
1750 North Vine
Hollywood, CA 90028
(213) 462-6252

CBS Records Incorporated
51 West 52nd Street
New York, NY 10019
(212) 975-4321

MCA
70 Universal City Plaza
Universal City, CA 91608
(818) 777-4000

Polygram Records
810 Seventh Avenue
New York, NY 10019
(212) 333-8000

RCA Records
1133 Avenue of the Americas
New York, NY 10036
(212) 930-4000

Warner Brothers Records
3300 Warner Boulevard
Burbank, CA 91510
(818) 846-9090

MOVIES AND MOVIE RATING (INCLUDING HOME VIDEOS)

The Motion Picture Association of America
1600 I Street, NW
Washington, DC 20006
(202) 293-1966

THE ADVERTISING INDUSTRY

The Advertising Council
825 Third Avenue
New York, NY 10022
(212) 758-0400

American Advertising Federation
1225 Connecticut Avenue, NW
Washington, DC 20036
(202) 659-1800

Television Bureau of Advertising
1345 Avenue of the Americas
New York, NY 10019
(212) 397-3458

SUICIDE

American Association of Suicidology
2459 S. Ash
Denver, CO 80222
(303) 692-0985

Educates the public on the subject through publications and programs.

International Association for Suicide Prevention
Suicide Prevention and Crisis Center
1811 Trousdale Drive
Burlingame, CA 94010
(415) 877-5604

Disseminates information about suicide and ar-
ranges for specialized training of persons on suicide
prevention.

National Committee on Youth Suicide Prevention
230 Park Avenue, Suite 835
New York, NY 10169
(212) 587-4998

Volunteer network of concerned parents and professional and government officials; assists in developing
youth suicide prevention programs in local communities.

National Save-A-Life League
4520 Fourth Avenue, Suite MH3
New York, NY 11220
(212) 492-4067

Youth Suicide National Center
1825 I Street, NW
Suite 400
Washington, DC 20006
(202) 429-2016

DUNGEONS AND DRAGONS

Bothered About Dungeons and Dragons, Inc.
P.O. Box 5513
Richmond, VA 23220
(804) 264-0403

Assists parents in dealing with children involved with the game Dungeons and Dragons

ALCOHOL AND DRUG ABUSE

Alcoholics Anonymous
Look up local chapters in telephone directory. For more information, contact the New York office: (212) 473-6200.

Al-Anon
Resource for children and families of alcoholics. For more information, look up local chapter in telephone directory or call the New York office: (212) 302-7240. Teenagers can call Alateen: (212) 254-7230.

National Clearinghouse of Alcohol Information
P.O. Box 2345
Rockville, MD 20852
(301) 468-2600

National Clearinghouse for Drug Abuse Information
P.O. Box 2305
Rockville, MD 20857
(301) 443-6500

National Council of Alcoholism
Publications Division
733 Third Avenue
New York, NY 10017

National Federation of Parents for Drug Free Youth
8730 Georgia Avenue, Suite 200
Silver Spring, MD 20910
(301) 585-5437

National Parent Resource Institute for Drug Education
Volunteer Service Center, Suite 1002
100 Edgewood Avenue, NE
Atlanta, GA 30303
(800) 241-7946

RELIGIOUS ORGANIZATIONS' MEDIA EDUCATION AGENCIES

American Baptist Churches in the USA
Parent Education
Educational Ministries
P.O. Box 851
Valley Forge, PA 19482

Church of the Nazarene
Sunday School and Christian Life Division
6401 The Paseo
Kansas City, MO 64131
(816) 333-7000

The Episcopal Church
Education for Mission and Ministry
Episcopal Church Center
815 Second Avenue
New York, NY 10017
(212) 867-8400

Lutheran Council in the USA
Lutheran Film Associates
360 Park Avenue, South
New York, NY 10010
(212) 532-6350

Media Action Resource Center
475 Riverside Drive
New York, NY 10115
(212) 865-6690

Presbyterian Church (U.S.A.)
Church Education Services
The Program Agency
475 Riverside Drive
New York, NY 10115
(212) 870-2757

Southern Baptist Convention
Christian Life Commission
901 Commerce Street
Nashville, TN 37203
(615) 244-2495

Union of American Hebrew Congregations
Division of Media and Communication
Department of Education
838 Fifth Avenue
New York, NY 10021
(212) 249-0100

United Church of Christ
Board for World Ministries
Division of Health and Welfare
475 Riverside Drive
New York, NY 10115
(212) 870-2637

The United Methodist Church
United Methodist Communications
Public Media Division
475 Riverside Drive
New York, NY 10115
(212) 663-8900

United States Catholic Conference
Department of Communication
1011 First Avenue
New York, NY 10022
(212) 644-1898

United Synagogue of America
Department of Education
155 Fifth Avenue
New York, NY 10010
(212) 533-7800

CANADA

Canadian Association of Broadcasters
P. O. Box 626
Station B
Ottawa, Ontario K1P 5F2
(613) 233-4025

Canadian Broadcasting Corporation
1500 Bronson Avenue
Ottawa, Ontario K1G 3J5
(613) 731-3111

CKO
30 Carlton Street
Toronto, Ontario M5B 2E9
(416) 591-1222

Canadian Radio-Television and Telecommunications Commission
Central Building
Promenade du Portage
Hull, Quebec K1A 0N2
(819) 997-0313

CTV Television Network, Ltd.
42 Charles Street East
Toronto, Ontario M4Y 1T5
(416) 928-6000

Global Television Network
81 Barber Greene Road
Don Mills, Ontario M3G 2A2
(416) 466-5311

TVA
1600 de Maisonneuve Boulevard East
Montreal, Quebec H2L 4P2
(514) 526-9251

Advertising Standards Council of Canada
350 Bloor Street East
Suite 402
Toronto, Ontario, M5W IH5

Association for Media Literacy
40 McArthur Street
Etobicoke, Ontario M9P 3M7

Canadian Coalition Against Violent Entertainment
1 Duke Street
Hamilton, Ontario L89 IW9
(416) 524-0508

Anglican Church of Canada
Family Ministries
Church House
600 Jarvis Street
Toronto, Ontario M4Y 2J6
(416) 924-9192

Canadian Conference of Catholic Bishops
National Office of Religious Education
90 Parent Avenue
Ottawa, Ontario K1N 7B1
(613) 236-9461

United Church of Canada
Division of Communications
85 St. Clair Avenue East
Toronto, Ontario M4T 1M8
(416) 925-5931

Notes

Introduction

1. Mötley Crüe, "Too Young to Fall in Love," *Shout at the Devil*, Elektra/Asylum 60289-1. Lyrics by Nikki Sixx. Lyrics copyright © 1983 Warner-Tamerlane Publishing Corp./Motley Crue Music.

Chapter 1

1. Statements by Wendy O. Williams made at the National Association of Recording Arts & Sciences forum, 10 September 1985.

2. Prince, "Darling Nikki," *Purple Rain*, Warner Brothers Records 1-25110. Warner Brothers Music Corp. Words and music by Prince. Copyright © 1984 Controversy Music.

3. National Coalition on TV Violence, "NCTV Musicvideo Report, Oct. '83-Nov. '84" (Champaign, Ill.: National Coalition on TV Violence, 1984).

4. "NAB Asks Labels To Send Song Lyrics To Stations With Records," *Radio & Records* (7 June 1985), p.11.

5. John Horn, "Rock Porn? Stations Are Warned," *Los Angeles Times*, 11 June 1985, sec. 6, p.1.

6. David Gergen, "X-Rated Records," *U.S. News & World Report* 98 (20 May 1985), p. 98.

7. Frank Zappa, " 'Extortion Pure And Simple. . . ' An Open Letter To The Music Industry," *Cash Box* 49 (31 August 1985), p. 3.

8. Marilyn Beck, "Motown great blasts porno on records, music videos," *New Orleans Times-Picayune/States-Item*, 22 July 1985, sec. C, p. 8.

9. "PRMC and National PTA Announce Coalition for Consumer Warning Labels and Explicit Lyrics," joint press release by the Parents' Music Resource Center and the National PTA, 11 September 1985.

10. Ibid.

11. Senate Committee on Commerce, Science, and Transportation, *Record Labeling*, 99th Cong., 1st sess., 1985.

12. Bob Guccione, Jr., "Who's Who, What's What, and Why," *SPIN* 2 (April 1986), p. 6.

13. Jamie Malanowski, "Tipper Gore's Diary," *SPIN* (January 1986), p. 82.

14. Max Kilmer, "Rock Lyric Rating Proposed," *Scholastic News* 48 (8 November 1985), pp. 1-2.

15. Barbara Jaeger, "Sex, Violence, and Rock 'n' Roll," *Denver Post*, 28 April 1985, sec. D., p. 18.

16. Ellen Goodman, "Little Madonnas," *Washington Post*, 8 June 1985, sec. A, p. 21.

17. Steve Gett, "Twisted Sister Achieve Success and Get Ready to Even Some Scores," *Metallion* 7, no. 2 (October-November 1984), p. 18.

18. "Record Lyrics Survey," from Simmons Market Research Bureau, Inc. (219 E. 42nd St., New York, N.Y. 10017), November 1985.

19. Walter Goodman, "Liberty Panel Ponders Wherefores of Freedom, *New York Times*, 7 July 1986.

Chapter 2

1. Ian Cranna, ed., *The Rock Yearbook 1986* (United Kingdom: Virgin Books, 1985), p. 104.

2. Steve Huntley and Harold Kennedy, "Expert Advice: Keep

Control of Family Fun," *U.S. News & World Report* 99 (28 October 1985), p. 54.

3. "Women Who Maintain Families," *Facts on U.S. Working Women*, U.S. Department of Labor, Women's Bureau, Fact Sheet no. 86-2, 1986.

4. Daniel P. Moynihan, *Family and Nation* (San Diego: Harcourt Brace Jovanovich, 1986), p. 46.

5. "Women Who Maintain Families," *Facts on U.S. Working Women*.

6. "Half of Mothers with Children Under 3 Now in Labor Force," *News*, Bureau of Labor Statistics, U.S. Department of Labor, 20 August 1986.

7. House Committee on Education and Labor, *School Facilities Child Care Act*, 98th Cong., 2nd sess., 1984, p. 33.

8. Business Advisory Commission of the Education Commission of the States, *Reconnecting Youth: The Next Stage of Reform*, October 1985, pp. 10, 13.

9. California Council on Criminal Justice, State Task Force on Youth Gang Violence, *Final Report*, January 1986, pp. 10-12.

10. P.E. Quinn, *Cry Out!* (Nashville: Abingdon Press, 1984), p. 183.

11. Mary Jordan, "Runaway Problem Spreads," *Washington Post*, 22 July 1985, sec. A, p. 1.

12. Jan Fowler, *Teenage Pregnancy: Statistics, Current Research, and Federal Legislation*, Congressional Research Service, 1 June 1982, p. 6.

13. Charlotte Ross, director of Youth Suicide National Center, telephone interview with author, September 1986.

Chapter 3

1. "An Exclusive Talk With A Shocking Performer—Blackie Lawless," *RockLine* (April 1985), p. 14.

2. Don Mueller, "The Lawless Brigade Take Metal Outrage To New Heights," *Hit Parader* (November 1985), p. 46.

3. W.A.S.P., "On Your Knees," WASP, Capitol/EMI ST-12343. Written by Blackie Lawless. Planetary Music Inc. Publishing controlled by Zomba Enterprises, Inc.

4. Kandy Stroud, "Stop Pornographic Rock," *Newsweek* (6 May 1985), p. 14.

5. Adrianne Stone, "W.A.S.P., Rock and Roll Outlaws," *Hit Parader* (January 1985), p. 56.

6. W.A.S.P., *Animal (F**k Like a Beast)*, Music for Nations 12-KVT-109.

7. Andy Secher, "The Kings of Shock Rock," *Hit Parader* (October 1985), p. 33.

8. Keith Greenberg, "W.A.S.P., Hot 'n' Nasty!" *Faces Rocks* (September 1985), p. 15.

9. Ibid, p. 17.

10. Ibid.

11. Mötley Crüe, "Live Wire," *Too Fast For Love*, Elektra/Asylum EI-60174. Written by N. Sixx. Published by Warner-Tamerlane Publishing Corp./Mötley Crüe Publishing.

12. Mötley Crüe, "Bastard," *Shout at the Devil*, Elektra/Asylum 60289-1. Lyrics by Nikki Sixx. Lyrics copyright © Warner-Tamerlane Publishing Corp./Motley Crue Music.

13. Carnivore, "Predator," *Carnivore*, Roadracer Records GWD90534. Written by Peter Steele. Published by Roadster Music.

14. Exciter, *Violence & Force*, Megaforce Records MRI 569.

15. Abattoir, *Vicious Attack*, Combat Records MX8014.

16. Savage Grace, *Master of Disguise*, Important Record Distributors RD-004.

17. Bitch, *Be My Slave*, Metal Blade MBR 1007.

18. Rolling Stones, *Undercover*, Rolling Stones Records RLS (S) 90120-1.

19. Dead Kennedys, "I Kill Children," *Fresh Fruit for Rotting Vegetables*, Cherry Red, C BRED 10. Written by Biafra. Copyright © 1980 Virgin Music (publishers) Ltd.

20. Slayer, "Kill Again," *Hell Awaits*, Combat/Metal Blade, MX8020. Lyrics by King. Published by Bloody Skull Music. Administered by Bug Music.

21. Jill Rosenbaum and Lorraine Prinsky, "Sex, Violence and Rock 'n' Roll: Youths' Perceptions of Popular Music." Paper delivered at annual meeting of the Western Society of Criminology, Newport Beach, Calif., February 1986; forthcoming in *Popular Music Society*.

22. Joe Stuessy, telephone interview with author, September 1985.

23. Joe Stuessy, quoted from Senate Committee on Com-

merce, Science, and Transportation, *Record Labeling,* 99th cong., 1st Sess., 1985, p. 117.

24. Ethlie Vare, "Molten Hot Metal Flares Anew In Fad-Defying Fling At Pop Success," *Billboard 96* (14 April 1984), p. HM-3.

25. Joe Stuessy, *The Heavy Metal User's Manual,* mimeographed handout, p.1. Available from Dr. Joe Stuessy, College of Fine Arts and Humanities, Division of Music, University of Texas at San Antonio, San Antonio, TX 78285.

26. Paul King, "Heavy Metal: A New Religion, *Journal of the Tennessee Medical Association* 78, no. 12 (December 1985), p. 755.

27. "Ax-Scissors death trial date slated," *Tacoma News Tribune,* 31 May 1986.

28. " 'Family hour' Aggression" *Knoxville Journal,* 11 September 1986, sec. A, p., 1.

29. Dr. George Gerbner, telephone interview with author.

30. Ibid.

31. Ibid.

32. Advertisement in *Electronic Media* (17 November 1986), p. 9.

33. Advertisement in *Electronic Media* (5 January 1987), p. 179.

34. "Lucky 13th," *Broadcasting* (15 September 1986), p. 6.

35. Nelson Price, "Pornography and Sexual Violence: Booming Business Victimizing Children, Women and Men," *Engage/ Social Action* (July/August 1985), p. 11.

36. Ibid.

37. "Cobra Revenge Violence & Poltergeist Satanic Horror Start Summer Season," National Coalition on Television Violence press release, 2 June 1986.

38. Barry L. Sherman and Joseph R. Dominick, "Violence and Sex in Music Videos: TV and Rock 'n' Roll," *Journal of Communication* (Winter 1986), pp. 90, 92.

39. National Coalition on TV Violence, "NCTV Musicvideo Report, Oct. '83–Nov. '84" (Champaign, Ill.: National Coalition on TV Violence, 1984).

40. Thomas Radecki, telephone interview with author.

41. Communications Commission, National Council of Churches of Christ in the U.S.A., "Violence and Sexual Violence in Film, Television, Cable and Home Video," photocopied report, 1985, p. 5.

42. Senate Committee on Commerce, *Television and Social*

Behavior, 92d. Cong., 2d sess., 21-25 March 1972.

43. Edward Donnerstein, "The Effects of Exposure to Violent Pornographic Mass Media Images," *Engage/Social Action* (July/August 1985), pp. 16-19.

44. Ibid., p. 16, 19.

45. Price, "Pornography and Sexual Violence," p. 13.

46. Ibid.

47. Communications Commission, National Council of Churches of Christ in the U.S.A., "Violence and Sexual Violence," p. 38.

48. "Children's aggression linked to TV Violence," *Rocky Mountain News,* 8 March 1985, sec. W, p. 35.

49. Thomas Radecki, telephone interview with author.

50. Senate Committee on Commerce, Science, and Transportation, *Record Labeling,* 99th Cong., 1st sess., 1985, p. 155.

51. Ibid.

52. Thomas Radecki, telephone interview.

53. Joe Stuessy, *Heavy Metal User's Manual,* p. 16.

Chapter 4

1. Prince, "Jack U Off," *Controversy,* Warner Brothers Records BSK3601. Written by Prince. Published by Controversy Music.

2. Sheena Easton, "Sugar Walls," *Private Heaven,* EMI America ST17132. Written by Alexander Nevermind. Copyright © Tionna Music.

3. Prince, "Sister," *Dirty Mind,* Warner Brothers Records BSK3478. Written by Prince. Published by Ecnirp Music Inc.

4. Vanity, "Nasty Girl," *Vanity 6,* Warner Brothers Records, 1-23716. Written by Prince. Published by Girl's Song Music.

5. Ted Nugent, "Wango Tango," *Scream Dream,* Epic FE36404. Written by Ted Nugent. Published by Magicland Music.

6. Frankie Goes to Hollywood, "Relax," *Welcome to the Pleasuredome,* Island Records 90232-1-H. Written by Frankie Goes to Hollywood. Published by Perfect Songs LTD. Administered by Island Music, Inc.

7. Vanity, "Ouch," *Skin on Skin*, Motown 6167ML. Written by Michael E. Dunlap, Tommy Faragher, Dennis Herring. Copyright © 1986 Zip Ya Lip Music/Citi Ave. Music.

8. Prince, "Erotic City," 45 RPM single, Warner Brothers, 7-2916.

9. Michael Goldberg, "Madonna Seduces Seattle," *Rolling Stone* (23 May 1985), p. 20.

10. Deborah Frost, "White Noise: How Heavy Metal Rules," *Village Voice* (18 June 1985), p. 47.

11. "Mötley Crüe," press release issued by Elektra/Asylum Records, September 1983.

12. J. Kordosh, "Sixx Things You Must Know About Motley Crue," *Creem* (November 1986), pp. 20-21.

13. Deborah Quilter, "The Health and Fitness of Rock 'n' Roll," *Bruce Jenner's Better Health and Living* (April 1986), p. 39.

14. Ted Nugent, "Violent Love," *Scream Dream*, Epic FE36404. Written by Nugent.

15. Mötley Crüe, "Tonight (We Need a Lover)," *Theater of Pain*, Elektra/Asylum 60418-1-E. Lyrics by N. Sixx. Copyright © 1985 Warner-Tamerlane Publishing Corp./Nikki Sixx Music/ Vince Neil Music.

16. Mötley Crüe, "Ten Seconds to Love," *Shout at the Devil*, Elektra/Asylum 60289-1. Lyrics by Nikki Sixx and Vince Neil. Lyrics copyright © 1983 Warner-Tamerlane Publishing Corp./ Mötley Crüe Music.

17. Kiss, "Fits Like a Glove," *Lick It Up*, Mercury 422-814297-1 M1. Written by Gene Simmons. Published by Kiss. Copyright © 1983 Kiss Organization Ltd.

18. The Who, "You Better You Bet," *Face Dances*, Warner Brothers Records HS3516. Written by Peter Townshend. Published by Towser Tunes, Inc.

19. AC/DC, "Let Me Put My Love into You" and "Shoot to Thrill," *Back in Black*, Atlantic SD16018. Written by Angus Young, Malcolm Young, and Brian Johnson. Published by J. Albert and Son Publishing, Ltd./E. B. Marks Music.

20. Judas Priest, "Eat Me Alive," *Defenders of the Faith*, Columbia Records, FC39219. Written by Glenn Tipton, Rob Halford, K. K. Downing. Copyright © 1984 April Music, Inc.; Crewglen Ltd.; Ebonytree Ltd.; Geargate Ltd. Administered by April Music, Inc.

21. Great White, "On Your Knees," *Great White*, EMI America ST 17111. Written by Kendall, Russell, Holland, Black, Dokken. Lyrics copyright © 1984 Great White.

22. Dokken, "Bullets to Spare," *Tooth and Nail*, Elektra/Asylum 60376-1. Written by Mick Brown, Don Dokken, George Lynch, Jeff Pilson. Published by Megadude Music; E/A Music, Inc.; Warner Brothers Music.

23. Joe Stuessy, telephone interview with author.

24. Ibid. Subsequent quotations from Stuessy in this chapter from this interview.

25. David Fahey, "Helmut Newton," *Interview* 16 (January 1986), p. 46.

26. "How to Get Attention: Let's Talk Dirty," *Newsweek* (19 May 1986), p. 60.

27. Jennet Conant, "Sexy Does It," *Newsweek* (15 September 1986), p. 63.

28. Ibid., p. 64.

29. Ronald Alsop, "Personal-Product Ads Abound As Public Gets More Tolerant," *Wall Street Journal*, 14 August 1986, p. 19.

30. "Who Has the Biggest Bulge in Rock?" *Metal Hotline* (August 1986), p. 42.

31. Mary Aloe, "Kinky Berlin," *Rock Magazine* 3 (May-June 1984), p. 37.

32. Andy Secher, "Mötley Crüe: The Sleaze Patrol," *Hit Parader* (June 1984), p. 16.

33. Andy Secher, "Mötley Crüe: The Wild Bunch," *Hit Parader* (August 1984), p. 20.

34. Andy Secher, "Mötley Crüe: Out for Blood," *Hit Parader* (December 1983), p. 36.

35. Harrison Donnelly, "Pornography: Setting New Limits," *Editorial Research Reports* 1, no. 18 (16 May 1986), p. 363.

36. Advertisement on file at the Parents' Music Resource Center. Kalbrus' address is 175 Fifth Ave., New York, NY 10010.

37. Claudia Wallis et al., "Children Having Children," *Time* (9 December 1985), p. 79.

38. Ibid., pp. 78-90.

39. David Gelman et al., "The Games Teen-Agers Play," *Newsweek* (1 September 1980), p. 48.

40. Jan Fowler, *Teenage Pregnancy: Statistics, Current Research, Federal Legislation*, Congressional Research Service, 1 June 1982, p. 6.

41. Jane Murray, "Teen Pregnancy: an international perspective," *Planned Parenthood Review* (Winter 1986), p. 20.

42. Jean Seligmann et al., "A Nasty New Epidemic," *Newsweek* (4 February 1985), p. 72.

43. Murray, "Teen Pregnancy," p. 20.

44. Nelson Price, "Pornography and Sexual Violence: Booming Business Victimizing Children, Women and Men," *Engage/ Social Action* (July/August 1985), p. 13.

Chapter 5

1. Elton John, "I Think I'm Going to Kill Myself," *Honky Chateau*, MCA 2017. Written by Elton John and Bernie Taupin. Copyright © Dick James Music Ltd.
2. Charlotte Ross, director of Youth Suicide National Center, telephone interview with author, September 1986.
3. Patricia McCormack, "High-Achieving Teen-Agers Tell of Considering Suicide," *Washington Post*, 14 September 1986, sec. A, p. 7.
4. Alfred B. DelBello, "Needed: A U.S. Commission on Teen-Age Suicide," *New York Times*, 12 September 1984, sec. A, p. 31.
5. Suicidal Tendencies, *Suicidal Tendencies*, Frontier FLP1011.
6. Accept, *Russian Roulette*, CBS BFR40354.
7. Suicidal Tendencies, "Suicide's an Alternative/You'll Be Sorry," *Suicidal Tendencies*, Frontier FLP1011. You'll Be Sorry Music. Copyright © 1983 American Lesion Music.
8. Suicidal Tendencies, "Memories of Tomorrow," *Suicidal Tendencies*, Frontier FLP1011. You'll Be Sorry Music. Copyright © 1983 American Lesion Music.
9. Suicidal Tendencies, "Suicidal Failure," *Suicidal Tendencies*, Frontier FLP1011. You'll Be Sorry Music. Copyright © 1983 American Lesion Music.
10. Metallica, "Fade to Black," *Ride the Lightning*, Elektra/ Asylum 60396-1. Written by Clifford Lee Burton, Lars Ulrich, Kirk L. Hammett, James Allen Hetfield. Lyrics copyright © 1984 Creeping Death Music.
11. Stewart Powell et al., "What Entertainers Are Doing to Your Kids," *U.S. News & World Report* (28 October 1985), p. 46.
12. "Ozzy Osbourne lyrics cited as cause in suicide," UPI, 13 January 1986.
13. Ozzy Osbourne, "Suicide Solution," *Blizzard of Oz*, Jet JZ 36812. Words and music by Ozzy Osbourne, Bob Daisley, Randy

Rhoads. Jet Music Ltd. Copyright © 1981 Essex Music International Ltd. TRO-Essex Music International, Inc., New York, controls all U.S.A. and Canada publication rights.

14. Richard de Atley, "Heavy Metal Singer Denies His Song Caused Suicide," AP, 21 January 1986.

15. Photograph in *Hit Parader* 42 (August 1983), p. 22. Credited to David McGough/DMI.

16. Jack McCollum, telephone interview with author.

17. Black Sabbath, "Killing Yourself to Live," *Sabbath Bloody Sabbath*, Warner Brothers BS2695. Written by Black Sabbath. Published by Rollerjoint Music.

18. Dan Peters and Steve Peters, *Why Knock Rock?* (Minneapolis: Bethany House Publishers, 1984), p. 157.

19. Allan Turner, "Heavy Metal: The hardest hard-rock sound is growing as a target of controversy," *San Antonio Light*, 22 September 1985, sec. M, p. 1.

20. Eugene Kane, "Medical examiner cites rock music in suicide," *Milwaukee Journal*, 11 February 1986, p. 1.

21. Michael Phillis, "Lawsuit: Rock lyrics led to youth's suicide," *Sparks Gazette Journal* (Nevada), 9 May 1986.

22. Ibid.

23. John Leo, "Could Suicide Be Contagious?" *Time* (24 February 1986), p. 59.

24. David L. Phillips and Lundie L. Carstensen, "Clustering of Teenage Suicides after Television News Stories about Suicide," *New England Journal of Medicine* 315 (11 September 1986), pp. 685-89.

25. Madelyn S. Gould and David Shaffer, "The Impact of Suicide in Television Movies," *New England Journal of Medicine* 315 (11 September 1986), pp. 690-94.

26. Sam Heys, "Is teenage suicide contagious?" *Atlanta Constitution*, 7 March 1986, sec. B, p. 1.

27. Conrad deFiebre, "Teen's suicide is fourth in Mankato in 3 1/2 months," *Minneapolis Star & Tribune*, 30 April 1986, sec. B, p. 1.

28. Annette Kornblum, "Pinpointing Youths At Risk for Suicide," *Washington Post*, 26 June 1985, p. 20.

29. Jack McCollum, telephone interview.

Chapter 6

1. "Paul McCartney: The Rolling Stone Interview," *Rolling Stone* (11 September 1986), p. 48.
2. Sandi Gallant, telephone interview with author, 23 September 1986. All subsequent Gallant quotations from this interview.
3. Joe Stuessy, telephone interview with author, September 1986. All subsequent quotations from Joe Stuessy in this chapter from this interview.
4. Grim Reaper advertisement, *Creem* (October 1984), p. 7.
5. *Congressional Record*, 99th cong., 1st sess., 26 September 1985, Vol. 131, no. 123, p. 3.
6. King Diamond quotation from Joe Stuessy, telephone interview, September 1986.
7. Venom, "Sacrifice," *Here Lies Venom*, Combat Records MX8062. Written by Dunn, Bray, Lant. Published by Neat Music. Licensed from Neat Records by Combat Records.
8. Venom, *Welcome to Hell*, Neat Records 1-002 LP.
9. Rich Stim, "Slayer," *SPIN* (September 1986), p. 32.
10. Anthony DeCurtis, "Record Label Gets Cold Feet, Won't Release Heavy Metal Album," *Rolling Stone* (9 October 1986), p. 20.
11. Slayer, "Necrophiliac," *Hell Awaits*, Combat/Metal Blade MX 8020. Lyrics and music by Hanneman and King. Published by Bloody Skull Music. Administered by Bug Music.
12. Cleo Wilson, telephone interview with author, September 1986. All subsequent quotations from Wilson from this interview.
13. Bill Wickersham, telephone interview with author, September 1986. All subsequent quotations from Wickersham from this interview.
14. Dann Cuellar, telephone interview with author, 6 September 1986. All subsequent quotations from Cuellar from this interview.
15. Wilson telephone interview.
16. Bill Solomon, telephone interview with author, 21 September 1986.

Chapter 7

1. Jodi Dorland, "Theater of Pain Rockets the Crue Back to the Top," *Hit Parader* (September 1985), p. 54.

2. Richard Harrington, "A 'Porn Lyric' Survey," *Washington Post*, 22 January 1986, sec. C, p. 7.

3. AC/DC, "Have A Drink On Me," *Back in Black*, Atlantic SD 16018. Written by Angus Young, Malcolm Young, and Brian Johnson. Published by J. Albert and Son Publishing, Ltd./E. B. Marks Music.

4. Ricki Wertz, "Are We Losing a Generation of Youth to Chemical Abuse?" *Engage/Social Action* (September 1985), p. 28.

5. Ibid.

6. Bureau of the Census, *Statistical Abstract of the United States, 1985* (Washington, 1985), p. 173.

7. Def Leppard, "High 'n' Dry (Saturday Night)," *High 'n' Dry*, Mercury SRM-1-4021. Written by Steve Clark, Joe Elliot, Rick Savage. Published by Zomba Enterprises, Inc.

8. "Van Halen: Diamond Dave Speaks Out," *Hit Parader* (July 1984), p. 33.

9. Journey, "Lay It Down," *Escape*, Columbia 37408. Written by S. Perry, N. Schon, J. Cain. Copyright © 1981 Weed High Nightmare Music. All administrative rights controlled by Screen Gems-EMI Music Inc.

10. "Mötley Crüe Speak Out," *Hit Parader* (March 1985), p. 54.

11. Album liner, Mötley Crüe, *Shout at the Devil*, Elektra/Asylum Records 60289-1.

12. *Kerrang!* (6 February 1986), p. 21.

13. *Kerrang!* no. 83 (13 December 1984), p. 25. Photo credited to Ross Halfin.

14. Tom Morganthau et al., "Kids and Cocaine," *Newsweek* (17 March 1986), p. 58.

15. Miller Newton, "New Jersey Opinion: New Approach to Drug Crisis," *New York Times*, 2 December 1984, sec. 11, p. 34.

16. "Heavy Metal Madness," *Tiger Beat* (January 1985), p. 24.

17. Tony Sanchez, *Up and Down with the Rolling Stones* (New York: W. Morrow, 1979), p. 257.

18. Mark Berry, "Another Stilled Voice: Drugs and Talent Don't Mix," *Billboard* (23 August 1986), p. 9.

19. Ibid.

20. Frank Spotnitz, "The Sex Pistols are dead, but Johnny Rotten is alive and well," UPI, 28 September 1984.

21. Melba Moore, "Performers Should Speak Out Against Drugs," *Billboard* 98 (20 September 1986), p. 9.

22. Steven Dupler, "RAD Kicks off Antidrug Campaign," *Billboard* (29 November 1986), p. 3.

23. Richard M. Smith et al., "Reagan: Drugs Are the 'No. 1' Problem," *Newsweek* (11 August 1986), p. 18.

24. Richard Harrington, "Rock With a Capital R and a PG-13," *Washington Post*, 15 September 1985.

25. Carl Spencer Taylor, interview with author, 3 July 1986. Subsequent quotations from Taylor in this chapter from this interview.

26. Peggy McCarthy, "A New Program to Treat Young Alcoholics," *New York Times*, 19 May 1985, sec. 11, p. 2.

27. George A. Hacker and Michael F. Jacobson, "Project SMART: Call for Time Out on 'Miller Time,' " *Engage/Social Action* (January 1985), p. 37.

28. Ann Landers' column, *Washington Post*, 14 September 1986.

29. National PTA Resolution, 1984.

30. Hacker and Jacobson, "Project SMART," p. 39.

31. Ibid.

32. Donald A. Moses and Robert Burger, *Are You Driving Your Children to Drink?* (New York: Van Nostrand Rienhold Company, 1975).

33. Lee Rank, "Making Living Enough of a High," *Christian Home* (October 1977), pp. 7-9.

Chapter 8

1. Bob Stewart, "Heavy metal shocks parent," *San Antonio Light*, 10 March 1985, sec. A, p. 1.

2. "Live Aid Concert Total Estimated at $70 Million," *New York Times*, 16 July 1985, sec. C, p. 16.

3. "ABC's 'Live Aid' Seen by 40 Million," *New York Times*, 17 July 1985, sec. C, p. 22.

4. Earl W. Foell, "Historic value of 'Live Aid' depends on follow-through," *Christian Science Monitor*, 16 July 1985, p. 3.
5. Rick Evans, "The Controversy Continues," *Hit Parader* (June 1984), p. 5.
6. Steve Gett, "Guitar Greats," *Hit Parader* (March 1984), p. 24.
7. John Branston, "Motley Rock," *Memphis Commercial Appeal Mid-South Magazine* (5 January 1986), p. 14.
8. Mötley Crüe, "Tonight (We Need A Lover)," *Theatre of Pain*, Elektra/Asylum 60418-1-E. Lyrics by Sixx. Copyright © 1985 Warner-Tamerlane Publishing Corp./Nikki Sixx Music/Vince Neil Music.
9. Barbara Jaeger, "Sex, Violence and Rock 'n' Roll," *Denver Post*, 28 April 1985, sec. D, p. 1.
10. Dwight Silverman, "Drugs, violence steal the show," *San Antonio Light*, 10 March 1985.
11. *Lizzy Borden Live: The Murderess Metal Show*. Metal Blade Video EVB-2001. Copyright © 1986 Bloody Skull Music. VHS videocassette.
12. Robert K. Oermann, "Alice Cooper continues his lock on shock rock," *Sunday Nashville Tennessean Showcase*, 28 December 1986, p. 24.
13. D. C. Denison, "The Interview," *Boston Globe Sunday Magazine*, 16 September 1985.
14. Carl Spencer Taylor, telephone interview with author, 3 July 1986.
15. Ibid.
16. Robert Palmer, "The Pop Life," *New York Times*, 6 January 1982, sec. C, p. 13.
17. "Rock Concert Rape," *Washington Post*, 31 December 1981, sec. A, p. 3.
18. Mary Schlangerstein, "Everybody came to have a good time," UPI, 7 December 1981.
19. Suzanne Daley, "Youth Gangs Rob Fans After Show," *New York Times*, 24 July 1983, sec. 1, p. 1.
20. "Regional News," UPI, Chalmette, Louisiana, 24 May 1984.
21. "Regional News," UPI, Arizona-Nevada, 20 December 1985.
22. "New York City Rock Concert Ends in Stabbings, Fights," Reuters North European Service, 28 December 1985.
23. "Boy accused of having sex at concert," *Milwaukee Journal*, 1 November 1985.

24. "Girl, 17, Raped During Show at Amphitheater," *Los Angeles Times*, 17 September 1985, Orange County edition, Metro section, p. 4.

25. "Regional News," UPI, Tacoma, Washington, 28 May 1986.

26. "Concertgoers Injured: Man dead, woman raped," *Detroit Free Press*, 29 May 1986.

27. "Youths go on a spree during Madison Square Garden concert," UPI, 9 June 1986.

28. "Man Dies From Injuries At Ozzy Concert," *Chattanooga Times*, 18 June 1986.

29. "Regional News," UPI, Pittsburgh, 1 July 1986.

30. Ellen M. Perlmutter, "Drugs, concert lyrics tied to rampage," *Pittsburgh Press*, 30 June 1986, p. 1.

31. "Regional News," UPI, Pittsburgh, 1 July 1986.

32. Irv Lichtman, "Inside Track," *Billboard* (8 November 1986), p. 84.

33. Sally Ann Stewart, "New music takes rap for gang violence," *USA Today*, 19 August 1986.

34. Irv Lichtmann, "Suit Targets Aerosmith," *Billboard* (6 December 1986), p. 82.

35. Carl S. Taylor, *Rock Concerts: A Parent's Guide* (Detroit:1984).

36. Ibid., p. 11.

37. Ibid., p. 14.

38. Ibid., p. 17.

39. Ibid.

40. Ibid.

Chapter 9

1. Beatles, "All You Need Is Love," *Magical Mystery Tour*, Capitol SMAL 2835. Written by John Lennon and Paul McCartney. Published by Maclen Music, Inc.

Conclusion

1. Michael Satchell, "Does Hollywood Push Drugs to Kids?" *Parade Magazine* (21 July 1985), p. 5.

2. Anthony DeCurtis, "Label Gets Cold Feet, Won't Release Heavy Metal Album," *Rolling Stone* (9 October 1986), p. 20. Slayer, *Reign in Blood*, Geffen Records GHS24131.

3. George D. Weiss, "Porn-rock: A Script For Censorship," *Billboard* 97 (29 June 1985).

4. "Paul McCartney: The Rolling Stone Interview," *Rolling Stone* (11 September 1986), p. 48.

Appendix A

1. Susie Phillips, "S.A. OKs music, theater foul language ordinance; first in U.S.," *San Antonio Express-News*, 15 November 1985, sec. A, p. 1.

2. Jim Michaels, "Psychiatrist for concert restrictions," *San Antonio Light*, 10 October 1985.

3. Ibid.

4. Bobbie Mueller, telephone interview with author, 26 September 1985.

Index

Index

Orbin, Jack, 173
Osbourne, Ozzy, 51, 106, 107, 112, 117, 125, 151
Osmond, Marie, 94
"Ouch," 84

"Panorama," 24
Parade Magazine, 166
Parents' call to action, 76-79
Parents in the community, 160
Parents' Music Resource Center (PMRC), 15, 19, 23-27, 32-34, 37, 58, 77, 91, 109, 112, 157, 166, 167, 169, 171
Pearl, David, 73
Pennsylvania State University, 75
Penthouse, 28, 34, 81
Perry, Ellis, 90, 92
Petric, John, 127
Petty, Tom, 71
Phillips, David P., 113
Photograph (video), 18
Pilpel, Harriet, 37
Pink Floyd (band), 58, 109, 112
Playboy, 28, 81
Poltergeist, 119
Porn rock versus hard-core pornography, 99-101
Porter, Bob, 15

Predator (album), 54
Predator (band), 50
Presley, Elvis, 83, 149
Prince, 17, 21, 82-84
Project SMART, 137
Pulling, Pat, 118
Purple Rain, 17

Quiet Riot (band), 130

Radecki, Thomas, 71, 75, 76
Radio and Records, 21
Rambo, 148
Raspberry, William, 23
RCA Records, 22, 118
Reagan, Ronald, 133
Recording Industry Association of America (RIAA), 22, 23, 25, 29, 30, 33, 34, 91, 163
Rehman, Sharas, 75
Reign in Blood, 120, 166
Reilly, Susan, 75
"Relax," 83
Ride the Lightning, 106
Ritchie, Lionel, 144
Robb, Charles, 45
Robinson, Smokey, 27, 82, 166
Rock Against Drugs (RAD), 132